Cognitive Behavioral
Approaches for Counselors

THEORIES FOR COUNSELORS SERIES

Cognitive Behavioral
Approaches for Counselors

Diane Shea
Holy Family University

Cognitive Behavioral
Approaches for Counselors

Diane Shea
Holy Family University

Los Angeles | London | New Delhi
Singapore | Washington DC | Boston

Los Angeles | London | New Delhi
Singapore | Washington DC | Boston

FOR INFORMATION:

SAGE Publications, Inc.

2455 Teller Road

Thousand Oaks, California 91320

E-mail: order@sagepub.com

SAGE Publications Ltd.

1 Oliver's Yard

55 City Road

London, EC1Y 1SP

United Kingdom

SAGE Publications India Pvt. Ltd.

B 1/I 1 Mohan Cooperative Industrial Area

Mathura Road, New Delhi 110 044

India

SAGE Publications Asia-Pacific Pte. Ltd.

3 Church Street

#10–04 Samsung Hub

Singapore 049483

Acquisitions Editor: Kassie Graves

Editorial Assistant: Carrie Montoya

Production Editor: Tracy Buyan

Copy Editor: Deanna Noga

Typesetter: Hurix Systems Pvt. Ltd.

Proofreader: Lawrence W. Baker

Indexer: Maria Sosnowski

Cover Designer: Anupama Krishnan

Marketing Manager: Shari Countryman

Printed in the United States of America

Library of Congress Cataloging-in-Publication Data

Shea, Diane.

Cognitive behavioral approaches for counselors / Diane Shea, Holy Family University.

pages cm. — (Theories for counselors series; volume II)

Includes bibliographical references and index.

ISBN 978-1-4522-8277-0 (pbk. : alk. paper)

1. Cognitive therapy. 2. Rational emotive behavior therapy. 3. Counselor and client. 4. Counseling. I. Title.

RC489.C63S54 2016

616.89'1425—dc23   2014042367

This book is printed on acid-free paper.

15 16 17 18 19 10 9 8 7 6 5 4 3 2 1

Brief Contents

Detailed Contents

Series Preface

"Theories for Counselors" provides practical applications of major theories from a common factors, multicultural perspective. What does that mean? Let's break it down.

The authors in the "Theories for Counselors" series are highly experienced counselors with extensive knowledge and expertise concerning the theory that they present. They present each theory from an applied perspective, asking themselves, "How is this concept useful in actual clinical practice?" It may surprise you to know this, but Freud's work can be (and is) applied day in and day out in modern counseling. (If this surprises you, it could indicate that you have not been taught Freud well.) He believed that the relationship between the client and clinician was of utmost importance; he believed that his patients needed to feel comfortable speaking their mind; he believed that clinicians needed to listen with attentiveness and tact. Freud's legacy, as is shown in the first book of this series, *Psychoanalytic Approaches for Counselors*, has been revised and revisited, but its therapeutic usefulness remains, and for each theory that is presented, therapeutic utility is utmost on the minds of the authors as they present material to their readers.

Each book begins by addressing the two most vital themes common to any counseling theory: the client and the therapeutic relationship. Why have we picked the client and the therapeutic relationship as the two most important themes? The reason is called the *common factors hypothesis*, and this is where research comes in. The common factor hypothesis is the result of decades of research that has compared various schools of counseling and psychotherapy. Contrary to prior belief, it has been convincingly demonstrated that research in general finds no significant difference in how effective the various therapies are. These findings, predicted by Rosenzweig (1936/2002) nearly 80 years ago, began to be empirically demonstrated in the mid-1970s (Luborsky, Singer, & Luborsky, 1975; Smith & Glass, 1977). Research confirming the relative equivalence of bona fide therapies has accumulated since that time (e.g., Ahn & Wampold, 2001; Lambert, 1992;

Lambert & Barley, 2001; Lambert & Ogles, 2004; Wampold, Mondin, Moody, Stich, Benson, & Ahn, 1997).

What does this mean? It means that instead of therapeutic improvement being due to specific ingredients prescribed by different theoretical schools of counseling and psychotherapy, positive therapeutic change can be attributed to factors that are common to all bona fide therapies. Additionally, these factors can be broken down into four categories: client variables (40% of change), relationship variables (30%), hope and expectancy (15%), and theory or technique (15%) (Duncan, 2002b; Lambert, 1992) (see Figure 1).

As we see, the client and the relationship account for the vast majority of therapeutic change, and as such, should be centrally located in the presentation of any counseling theory.

Interestingly, the history of counseling begins right where research predicts: in an intense relationship between one person who wants help and another person wanting to help. Sigmund Freud, who inaugurated themes that continue to organize the counseling profession, described and redescribed the origins of psychoanalysis. Two major components in his descriptions were the famous first patient of psychoanalysis, Bertha Pappenheim (referred to in case studies as "Anna O."), and the relationship she had with her doctor, Josef Breuer, Freud's friend and colleague at the time. Though Freud revised his opinions on many things about that famous case (as he did about almost everything), what remained constant was the fact that he saw something of primary importance in that case—the "talking cure" that occurs between a patient/client and doctor/counselor.

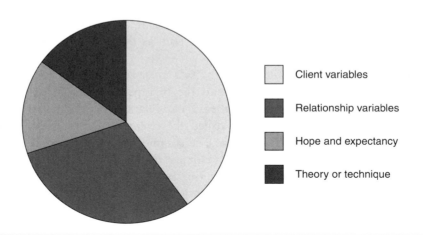

Figure 1   Common Factors

Source: Lambert, M. J. (1992). Psychotherapy outcome research: Implications for integrative and eclectic therapists. In J. C. Norcross & M. R. Goldfried (Eds.), *Handbook of psychotherapy and behavior change* (4th ed., pp. 143–189). New York, NY: John Wiley.

Thus the origins of counseling display a deep consonance with the latest in empirical research, and it is this consonance that is the underlying theme behind the series "Theories for Counselors." Starting with Freud and moving through past and contemporary counseling theories and theorists, the focus remains on the client and the therapeutic relationship, and how this relationship fosters and enhances the client's natural resilience and hope for change. The theory's techniques and the theory itself are important only inasmuch as they provide a common roadmap—a way for both client and counselor to think about where a client has been and where he or she wants to go.

Just as it is important to know that Freud remains useful for contemporary counselors, so it is important to know that Freud began his work against a backdrop of rising racial hatred in Austria and Western Europe, and that while he successfully fled to England in 1938, his sisters perished in the Nazi concentration camps during the Holocaust (Gay, 2006). Thus the counseling enterprise began at a time of extreme racial hatred, which is a sobering and important fact to reflect on; from the inception of counseling in Western Europe and throughout its development worldwide, multicultural awareness and respect for diversity are no mere add-ons but are integral components for the practice of counseling. In addition, another important group membership—gender—has assumed greater and greater importance in the counseling field; its central importance imbued the case of Bertha Pappenheim, which has been deemed the founding one for psychoanalysis and hence for all that followed.

Counselors must practice from a culturally aware place rather than one that would seek to downplay the impact of race, gender, and other important group affiliations on our clients' lives. Sue, Arredondo, and McDavis (1992) provided a conceptual framework for organizing the types of competencies needed by a culturally skilled counselor, saying that he or she becomes aware of his or her own assumptions, actively attempts to understand differing worldviews, and actively develops culturally sensitive intervention strategies and skills. Sue (2001) expanded his conceptual framework into a multidimensional model of cultural competence; this model was primarily focused on racial and ethnic minority groups, though he did also recognize that it might be applicable for other groups including those of "gender, sexual orientation, and ability/disability" (p. 816). Such topics are now recognized as rightfully fitting within the context of multicultural counseling (Conyers, 2002; Pope, 2002; Richardson & Jacob, 2002). In addition, Smith and Richards (2002) point out the obligation that counselors have to address issues of religion and spirituality as multicultural issues.

D'Andrea and Daniels (2001) provided a multicultural framework for working with clients that is RESPECTFUL and inclusive of Religion and spirituality, Economic class, Sexual identity, Psychological development, Ethnic/racial identity, Chronology, Trauma, Family, Unique physical abilities and disabilities, and Language and location of residence. Similarly, Hays (1996) outlined a model that emphasized nine cultural influences in relation to specific minority groups that counselors should be ADDRESSING: Age, Developmental and other Disabilities, Religion, Ethnicity/race, Social status, Sexual orientation, Indigenous heritage, and Gender. These models help counselors deliver diversity competent services and pay attention to all the potential resources that a client brings to the counseling encounter. Ultimately, respect for diversity and celebration of all aspects of culture and group membership should lead to a more nuanced understanding of the client and the sometimes-hidden strengths that he or she possesses. Better knowing a client enhances the richly relational counseling encounter that began with Freud's work.

Once again, this is consonant with the common factors approach. The common factors approach can be applied to, and makes sense of, any counseling theory, beginning with Freud and psychoanalysis. According to this approach, all bona fide counseling theories do the same thing, though they describe it using differing terminology. One analogy is traveling to a particular destination, say New York City. There is no one right way to get there—it depends on where you are starting from, whether you want to fly, drive, or take the train, and whether you want to get there by a direct route or take a scenic one. Each unique route is analogous to a different counseling theory. The destination is the same—in a travel scenario, getting to New York City, and in a counseling scenario, achieving positive treatment outcome.

In their book, *The Heroic Client*, Duncan and Miller (2000) put it this way—they seek to "(1) enhance those factors across theories that account for successful outcome; (2) encourage the client's unique integration of different theories; and (3) selectively apply diverse ideas and techniques as they are seen as relevant by the client" (p. 146). Miller has talked about the need for clinicians to know different theories because they serve as language resources to connect with the client. In this view, theory is a way to connect with clients; if one language that I'm using—for instance, solution focus therapy—doesn't appear to be the language that the client is speaking, then I should use other theoretical languages that might allow me to communicate better with my client. The test of the theory is in how well it accords with each individual client's culturally influenced worldview and how useful it proves to be in the context of the therapeutic encounter.

"Theories for Counselors" will help you consider theories from the perspective of the client and what makes sense to her or him. It will show that theory and technique are good inasmuch as they aid clients in understanding their present situation and what they need to do to improve it. Finally, the series will help you situate the work of counseling within a sociocultural framework that takes into account client uniqueness, universality, and important group affiliations to enhance and activate client resources.

A BRIEF PRIMER ON THE COMMON FACTORS: HYPOTHESIS

- Suspecting that there were characteristics that all effective therapies (and therapists) shared, Rosenzweig (1936/2002) makes the claim that there are common factors upon which good counseling rests, regardless of theoretical orientation.
- Researching further, scholars use meta-analysis—a summary about relevant empirical studies or an "analysis of analyses"—as a tool to compare treatment outcome studies.
- Gaining consensus from these meta-analytic studies, researchers suggest that positive therapeutic treatment outcome is due to the following four groups of factors:

  1. Client/extratherapeutic factors: 40%

  2. Therapeutic relationship factors: 30%

  3. Placebo/expectancy for change/hope: 15%

  4. Theory/technique: 15%

  (Duncan, 2002a)

- Correcting the above breakdown, later researchers suggest that while the common factors hypothesis has been supported—"these shared, curative factors drive the engine of therapy" (Hubble, Duncan, Miller, & Wampold, 2010, p. 28)—it has been somewhat oversimplified. The factors aren't discrete but are complexly interrelated.
- Focusing on effective therapists rather than effective therapies should be emphasized, since there are large differences in effectiveness among clinicians, and "Using formal client feedback to inform, guide, and evaluate treatment is the strongest recommendation" that came from a comprehensive update of common factors (Hubble et al., 2010, p. 424).
- Condensing this into a sentence, it means that from a common factors perspective, counselors use a theoretical roadmap—i.e., employing language that makes sense to the client—that helps to activate dormant client resources and enhance client hope and expectancy for change, within the context of a therapeutic relationship that "is characterized by trust, warmth, understanding, acceptance, kindness, and human wisdom" (Lambert & Ogles, 2004, p. 181) and that can allow for modifications and changes based on feedback from the client.

Finally, I direct the reader to the companion website for this book and series, http://study.sagepub.com/theoriesforcounselors. There you will find extended discussions of topics that are mentioned briefly in the text, topics that are not addressed in the text but that might be useful to know when studying for comprehensive or licensing exams, definitions of terms, and supplemental exercises and activities. In general, if a topic is not covered or is covered in detail in the printed text, please search the website, as it will in all likelihood be discussed there.

Acknowledgments

I first want to thank Fred Redekop for his invitation to be part of this endeavor. He encouraged and challenged me throughout the process of writing. Likewise, I am grateful for the help of my former student and research assistant, Barb Bisch. She is a counselor with great potential, and I look forward to seeing her make her own contributions to the field. I cannot forget the library staff at Holy Family. They were invaluable. In particular, Debby Kramer, who helped me track down hard-to-find original articles and books, while Chris Runowski and Kathy Kindness were always offering assistance and support. Finally, the folks at SAGE were wonderful to work with. Carrie Montoya, our editorial assistant, and Deanna Noga, copy editor, helped me with the final touches. An additional thanks to my friends and colleagues who gave me confidence that I could see this to completion!

Publisher's Acknowledgments

SAGE gratefully acknowledges the contributions of the following reviewers:

Carol Kottwitz DNP, ARNP
Gonzaga University

Kathleen R. Tusaie PhD, APRN-BC
The University of Akron, College of Health Professions, School of Nursing

Stephen Sidorsky, LCSW
Adjunct Instructor
Rutgers University School of Social Work

My family, friends, and many, many coworkers and students have inspired me and encouraged me over the years. I dedicate this book to you who have taught me that relationship is the common factor in life that can promote compassion and community.

Introduction

Recently I had the opportunity to participate in the 46th Annual Convention of the Association for Behavioral and Cognitive Therapies (ABCT). In one of the panel discussions, experts from various approaches to cognitive and behavioral therapies acknowledged that overzealous alliance to specific treatment interventions might even inadvertently lead to adverse effects with certain clients. Since the panelists acknowledged that many of the interventions were found to be equally effective, their discussion focused on searching for common ground. One panelist remarked that the interpersonal alliance is crucial. I agree. My suggestion is that **the most essential common ground** in all cognitive and behavioral approaches is the counselor's relationship with the client.

In this book, I introduce prospective counselors to Rational Emotive Behavior Therapy (REBT) as developed by Albert Ellis in the mid-1950s and Cognitive Behavioral Therapy (CBT) as developed by Aaron Beck in the early 1960s. I emphasize that the focus of REBT/CBT has always been on the client and the quality of the counseling relationship. These are paramount, even though some critics of REBT/CBT have suggested that the therapeutic relationship has often been overlooked or underemphasized. In contrast, I argue that, in fact, Ellis and Beck have added unique perspectives to our understanding of the therapeutic relationship. I begin by presenting a brief historical background sketch for REBT and CBT.

Albert Ellis and REBT

Son of Jewish parents, founder of REBT, Albert Ellis was born in Pittsburgh, Pennsylvania, on September 27, 1913. In his autobiography, Ellis (2010) described his mother as an incessant talker and his father as a successful salesman. He had two younger siblings, a brother 19 months younger and a sister born when he was 4 years old. At age 4 the family moved to New York City, where he was raised. Ellis first received a Bachelor of Business Administration in 1934 from New York's City College. He then studied clinical psychology in New York's Columbia University, where he received his MA in 1943 and his PhD in 1947.

Initially, Ellis was trained to counsel persons with family, marital, and sexual issues. Not satisfied with this, he began intensive training in psychoanalysis. Although he admitted early on that he had serious reservations about Freud's theory of personality, he continued to practice classical psychoanalysis. But, in his own words, while he enjoyed picking the brains of his patients to uncover hidden meanings in their dreams, he mused, "I soon found, alas, that I had to honestly admit to myself (and sometimes the patient as well) that I was usually dead wrong about this" (Ellis, 1962, p. 6). This caused Ellis to modify his approach to psychoanalysis. He became much more eclectic and actively engaged with his clients. However, he continued to become frustrated with patients who refused to take steps to alleviate their fears. He then turned to more behaviorist notions.

Exploring the notions of deconditioning as espoused by such psychotherapists as Wolpe and Salter, Ellis began to incorporate risk-taking activities with his patients, encouraging them to do the things they may actually fear. However, when a patient suggested that she or he may have been conditioned in early childhood to fear rejection by her or his parents, the patient might not actually overcome the fear. In other words, a patient's insight into his or her behavior didn't necessarily bring about change. This led Ellis to explore the question of why patients held on to illogical fears. He developed the idea that language and self-talk contributed to the development and maintenance of neurosis. By this time, Ellis considered himself a rational therapist and incorporated his insights into his private practice and delivered his first of a series of papers on rational therapy to the psychological community in 1955.

In 1959, Ellis founded his own institute, the renowned not-for-profit Institute for Rational-Emotive Therapy. By 1964, the Institute had grown and Ellis purchased a building in Manhattan, New York, which is today the Albert Ellis Institute.

Over the years, Ellis was a prolific writer and lecturer and sought after psychotherapist. He served as the president of the American Psychological Society's (APA) Division of Consulting Psychology as well as the Society for the Scientific Study of Sexuality. He also served on the board of many professional societies. Over his lifetime, Ellis published over 800 scientific papers and edited or authored over 75 books and 200 audio and video cassettes. He received numerous distinguished awards as a prominent psychologist, and in 1971, he was honored by the American Humanist Association as the Humanist of the Year. Ellis died at home on July 24, 2007.

Aaron Beck and CBT

Nearly 9 years Ellis's junior, Aaron Beck was born in Providence, Rhode Island, on July 18, 1921. He graduated from Brown University in 1942 and went on to study at Yale, where he earned his medical degree. Like Ellis, Beck was trained in psychoanalysis. He was a graduate of the Philadelphia Psychoanalytic Institute. From 1950 to 1952, he worked at the Austen Riggs Psychoanalytic Institute and spent much of his early career practicing classical psychoanalysis. As Beck recalled, by 1956, he ventured out to scientifically validate some of the psychoanalytic concepts of depression (Beck, Rush, Shaw, & Emery, 1979). This led to the development of what is known today as cognitive behavioral therapy (CBT).

By 1994, Aaron Beck and his daughter Judith Beck founded the Beck Institute for Cognitive Behavior Therapy as a nonprofit 501(c)(3) in Bala Cynwyd, Pennsylvania. The institute has become an international training center providing CBT workshops and consultation worldwide.

Like Ellis, Beck is a prolific writer. His publications include some 600 scholarly articles and 25 books. In addition, he has developed widely used assessment scales. Beck has also received numerous awards, including the Lasker-DeBakey Clinical Medical Research Award for his creation of cognitive therapy. He is an Honorary President of the Academy of Cognitive Therapy and a fellow of the American Academy of Arts and Sciences. Presently, Beck serves as President Emeritus of the Beck Institute.

New Perspectives on the Therapeutic Relationship

But why focus on the relationship? Is there evidence the therapeutic alliance or relationship is central to client improvement? Horvath and Symonds (1991) set out to examine this question. The results of their meta-analysis of 24 studies suggested that the quality of the therapeutic alliance as indicated by the clients' ratings was the best predictor of successful treatment. Ten years later, in a much larger meta-analysis, these two authors along with two other colleagues concluded that independent of how the alliance was measured or what therapeutic approach was involved, "The quality of the alliance *matters*" (Horvath, Del Re, Flückiger, & Symonds, 2011, p. 13).

Wampold (2010) further explained that from the common factors perspective, regardless of the specific theoretic approach to treatment, there are common factors that are "responsible for psychotherapeutic benefits rather than the ingredients to the particular theories" (p. 23). In the 1970s, researchers (Garfield, 1973; Garfield & Bergin, 1971; Strupp, 1973b) had been examining outcomes in psychotherapy in attempts to uncover the basic ingredients or common factors. Over a number of years these factors have been elaborated. Presently, authors (e.g., Duncan, 2002b; Lambert, 1992; Lambert & Barley, 2001) have pointed out that specific treatment techniques accounted for only 15% of treatment success, whereas the therapeutic alliance account for twice this, or 30% of the success. Factors outside counseling, that is, client variables, account for 40% of client improvement, and the hope or expectancy to improve, sometimes referred to as the *placebo effect*, account for another 15%.

While the common factors hypothesis has been gaining consensus in modern times, as Duncan (2002b) pointed out, these notions can be traced back to a classic article that was written in 1936 by Saul Rosenzweig. Rosenzweig (1936/2002) recognized that every theoretical approach to psychotherapy has merit. He metaphorically borrowed from a scene in *Alice in Wonderland* and declared, "At last the Dodo said, 'Everybody has won, and all must have prizes'" (p. 412). Following this, it seems logical that a more efficacious approach to counseling and therapy would be to develop treatments that are grounded in these common factors (Grencavage & Norcross, 1990), and in a recent interview with Lynne Shallcross (2012), Brad Elford pointed out that counselors should be mindful of each of these common factors if they want to help clients succeed. I do the same throughout this book.

But what prize is in store for REBT/CBT? I invite you, prospective counselors, to understand how the two giants of REBT/CBT, Ellis and Beck, both trained as psychoanalysts, added unique understandings to the meaning of self-acceptance and unconditional positive regard within the context of the therapeutic relationship in a different form of talk therapy.

In the first chapter, "Client and Relationship in REBT/CBT," I focus more specifically on the client-counselor relationship and how it has been assessed and defended despite criticisms that REBT/CBT counselors often may seem to deemphasize its importance. I look at specific client factors that may contribute to REBT/CBT's success or failure. I also discuss some of the challenges inherently related to REBT/CBT when counselors are too wedded to the medical model and give themselves an aura of scientific authority. Ellis (1977a) poked fun at this when he said that "presumably intelligent men and women, with hell knows how many academic degrees behind them (which we may unhumorously refer to as degrees of restriction rather than degrees of freedom), consistently take themselves too seriously" (p. 60).

In the second chapter, "Basic Tenets of REBT/CBT," I provide a description of the basic tenets of REBT and CBT, suggesting similarities and differences. I rely on primary sources of Ellis and Beck as well as other experts in the field of CBT. I provide clinical vignettes and excerpts from verbatim counseling sessions that demonstrate how a client is led to challenge unhealthy beliefs that underlie disturbed emotions. This is often done through self-monitoring of negative thoughts and homework assignments. Two unique techniques that REBT often uses are rational-emotive imagery and shame-attacking exercises. I provide readers with examples and challenge them to practice a "shame-attack."

In the third chapter, "Evolution of REBT/CBT," I focus on some "third-wave" therapies, which are considered under the umbrella of CBT. After World War II, there was a great need for more effective treatments for soldiers coming back from combat. This coincided with developments in the field of psychology where B. F. Skinner focused on the understanding of operant conditioning as a basis of behavior. Behaviorism developed as a "first wave" challenge to the traditional psychoanalytic therapy of Sigmund Freud. Later, in the 1960s, Ellis and Beck shifted attention to the role of cognitions in understanding human emotions and behavior. This was considered the "second wave" challenge to psychoanalysis. Now, 50 years later, there has been much growth and development in the field of REBT/CBT. The question has shifted to reexamining whether or not counselors should help clients control their thoughts or simply accept them. This has led to a "third wave" of cognitive therapies. Readers are introduced to (a) mindfulness-based cognitive therapy, (b) dialectical behavioral therapy, and (c) acceptance and commitment therapy. I cite research demonstrating the effectiveness of each of these and emphasize the importance of the therapeutic relationship for each. This chapter ends with a discussion of how neurobiological developments are impacting the understanding of many areas of mental health.

In the fourth chapter, "Multiculturalism," I describe how I believe a culturally competent, contemporary counselor, who is a proponent of REBT/CBT, would integrate multicultural adaptations into his or her practice. I base this description on 10 steps outlined by Hays (2009):

1. Assessing the person's and family's needs with an emphasis on culturally respectful behavior.

2. Identifying culturally related strengths and supports.

3. Clarifying what part of the problem is primarily environmental (i.e., external to the client) and what part is cognitive (internal) with attention to cultural influences.

4. For environmentally based problems, focus on helping the client make changes that minimize stressors, increase personal strengths and supports, and build skills for interacting more effectively with the social and physical environment.

5. Validate clients' self-reported experiences of oppression.

6. Emphasize collaboration over confrontation, with attention to client-counselor differences.

7. With cognitive restructuring, question the helpfulness (rather than the validity) of the thought or belief.

8. Do not challenge core cultural beliefs.

9. Use the client's list of culturally related strengths and supports to develop a list of helpful cognitions to replace the unhelpful ones.

10. Develop weekly homework assignments with an emphasis on cultural congruence and client direction.

In the fifth chapter, I begin with a case illustration that demonstrates how a counselor might approach a client using REBT/CBT but all the while being sensitive to developing a therapeutic alliance. I also show how REBT/CBT can be tailored for use with children and adolescents. Scripts are provided for a number of concrete exercises that are easily adapted and modified depending on the developmental level of the child.

Finally, in the sixth chapter, I conclude with the reminder that the founders of REBT/CBT really did focus on the relationship they had with their clients. It was, in fact, by taking seriously their clients' concerns about traditional psychoanalysis that REBT/CBT evolved. However, counselors who wish to practice REBT/CBT need not take on the persona of the founders. What they need to do is make sure they don't neglect the therapeutic relationship; however, it may find final expression.

Because humor in various forms has been interwoven into REBT/CBT, I end some chapters with one of Ellis's Rationally Humorous songs. These songs show how humor can challenge unhelpful thoughts and patterns, in part by highlighting incongruities and contradictions expressed by clients.

SAGE was founded in 1965 by Sara Miller McCune to support the dissemination of usable knowledge by publishing innovative and high-quality research and teaching content. Today, we publish more than 750 journals, including those of more than 300 learned societies, more than 800 new books per year, and a growing range of library products including archives, data, case studies, reports, conference highlights, and video. SAGE remains majority-owned by our founder, and after Sara's lifetime will become owned by a charitable trust that secures our continued independence.

Los Angeles | London | Washington DC | New Delhi | Singapore | Boston

1

Client and Relationship in REBT/CBT

In the early 1960s, Hobbs (1962) observed that the therapeutic relationship provides the initial resource for clients as they seek to progress in treatment. Later, Strupp (1973a) outlined what he believed to be the essential elements that were necessary for therapeutic changes to occur: developing a helping relationship, patterned on the relationship between parent and child and characterized by positive feelings such as "respect, interest, understanding, tact, maturity" (p. 1); influencing the client through the helping relationship and using various means such as suggestions and encouragement; and depending on the client's "capacity and willingness to profit from the experience" (p. 1).

Examining 50 publications for commonalities among various forms of psychotherapy, Grencavage and Norcross (1990) suggested that although there were diverse factors that had been posited, the therapeutic alliance was the one most frequently endorsed. Another meta-analysis (Horvath & Symonds, 1991) reviewing 24 studies confirmed the same. It was the quality of the therapeutic or working alliance that was positively related to progress in therapy. While there is controversy in some meta-analytic findings (Stiles, Shapiro, & Elliott, 1986), there is ample evidence that the majority of variance in treatment outcome can be attributed to the therapeutic alliance (Duncan, 2002a; Flückiger, Del Re, Wampold, Symonds, & Horvath, 2012; Lambert, 2005; Lambert & Barley, 2001; Martin, Garske, & Davis, 2000). In this chapter, I now focus more specifically on the client-counselor relationship and how it has been assessed and defended despite criticism from researchers such as Mahoney and Gabriel (1987) that counselors trained in rational emotive behavior therapy (REBT) and/or cognitive behavioral therapy (CBT) often may deemphasize their importance and focus more on teaching clients how to change their thoughts.

The Therapeutic Alliance

The notion of a therapeutic relationship can be traced back to the Greek physician Hippocrates, who believed that this relationship was the key to a patient being healed (Gilbert & Leahey, 2007). It was important over 2,000 years ago, and it is still important today. But what does the term *therapeutic alliance* or *relationship* imply? To understand this concept, it is necessary to briefly consider the fact that the concept of the therapeutic alliance emerged from the writings of Freud (Summers & Barber, 2003).

Freud believed that in psychoanalysis the patient would need to develop affectionate feelings toward the counselor that were derived from trusting parental relationships. Freud (1909–1910/1961) stated, "In every psycho-analytic treatment of a neurotic patient the strange phenomenon that is known as 'transference' makes its appearance. The patient, that is to say, directs toward the physician a degree of affectionate feelings (mingled, often enough, with hostility) which is based on no real relation between them and which . . . can only be traced back to old wishful phantasies of the patient's which have become unconscious. Thus the part of the patient's emotional life which he can no longer recall to memory is re-experienced by him in his relation to the physician" (pp. 56–57). In other words, the therapeutic relationship stimulates old patterns of behaviors that have their roots in the parent/child relationship. Similar notions of transference and countertransference as the basis of the alliance are found throughout psychoanalytic literature (Greenson, 1965; Sterba, 1934).

Bordin (1979), himself coming from the psychoanalytic tradition, reformulated this understanding. Bordin argued that not only does a psychoanalytic approach to therapy rely on this relationship, but also all forms of psychotherapy have the therapeutic relationship as central to helping a client change or grow. Bordin moved the notion of the therapeutic alliance from a psychodynamic notion to one that is considered pantheoretical (in other words, applicable to all counseling theories). For Bordin, there are three components that are necessary for a therapeutic alliance. First, it is an agreement that encompasses *bond* between the client and the counselor. This bond is understood as an overarching concept that taps into attachments between the counselor that is built on notions of trust, acceptance, and confidence. Second, it implies a mutually respectful partnership in which both the counselor and client seek consensus regarding the *goals* of therapy. Both the counselor and client agree on the outcome(s) for which interventions are aimed. Third, it involves an agreement between them on the means or *tasks* that will help the client achieve those goals. This includes in-counseling behaviors. Both the client and the counselor need to agree that the tasks are efficacious and both accept the responsibility. I am approaching the therapeutic alliance in REBT/CBT from this perspective. I show that all three components—bond, goals, and tasks—are taken very seriously in REBT/CBT therapy.

As I pointed out in the introduction, most alliance researchers have come to the conclusion that it is not the differences in therapeutic techniques that really matters (Stiles, Shapiro, & Elliott, 1986). Rather, the quality of the therapeutic alliance is actually the best predictor of successful treatment.

Bonds, Goals, and Tasks

To begin, Beck, Rush, Shaw, and Emery (1979) acknowledged that in person-centered Rogerian therapy, the notions of unconditional positive regard, genuineness, and empathy are central interrelated attitudes that all counselors need to adopt. I suggest that they were correct when they maintained that cognitive behavioral counselors must develop these same qualities as well—but within a slightly different framework. In building basic trust, the REBT/CBT counselor must learn to balance the need for a client to be autonomous with the need for structure.

Alford and Beck (1997) emphasized that to understand the therapeutic alliance from a cognitive perspective the focus must be on the collaborative nature of the relationship. This interaction between the counselor and the client is the primary principle of cognitive therapy: "The more a therapist and patient work together, the greater the learning experience for both. The joint effort not only engenders a cooperative spirit but also a sense of exploration and discovery" (Beck et al., 1979, p. 32). He termed this *collaborative empiricism* (Beck, 1976; Beck et al., 1979). He emphasized that there is a deliberate and conscious attempt to be active and engaging with the client to collaborate in developing treatment goals. In the therapeutic relationship, the counselor hypothesizes about a client's dysfunctional beliefs and then systematically tests the validity of these.

Tee and Kazantzis (2011) provided an example of such collaborative empiricism. In their scenario, the client states, "I don't want to go to dinner; people never talk to me—they think that I am boring" to which the therapist replies, "That sounds like a tricky situation for you. Would you like to talk about that some more?" The therapist goes on to demonstrate collaboration in the following way:

Therapist: Ok, well, if I am hearing you correctly, a concern that you have is that people think you are boring, and this is connected to your conversations with people. It might help us to find out under which situations this happens the most. . . . For the moment, I wonder what might be the reasons that people (including you) might not talk much sometimes?

Client: Gee, well, I don't know. . . . Perhaps they are tired . . . maybe, even they are waiting for a lead from someone else? Is it possible they think I don't make much of an effort?

Therapist: Those sound like some good possibilities. I really like how you are looking around the situation from different perspectives. I wonder how could we figure out how much of the "not talking" is due to other people's views of you . . . or any of those other ideas you have generated?

Client: Hmmm. Maybe I could take more notice what happens when I am socializing. . . .

Therapist: Good, let's figure out how to be specific about how you will notice that. . . . (p. 48)

As illustrated by this scenario, the counselor needs to be active but should not do for the client what the person can do for herself or himself. This is truly putting the relationship in perspective. In other words, the counselor cares enough to help the client become capable of standing on her or his own feet.

For an REBT/CBT counselor, acceptance does not mean that the counselor approves of everything that a client does, but the counselor assumes a nonjudgmental stance. In this vein, Ellis (Dryden & Ellis, 2001; Ellis, 2004) always emphasized the importance of what he called unconditional self-acceptance (USA), unconditional other-acceptance (UOA), and unconditional life acceptance (ULA). I propose that assuming these attitudes toward a client unequivocally demonstrates a genuine concern for the person.

To understand USA, a person is challenged to accept himself or herself with all his or her "warts and flaws" (Ellis, 2004, p. 173), while at the same time working hard to dispute and change self-defeating behaviors. Ellis contended that often in client-centered therapy, a client in turn learns to accept himself or herself *because* the counselor has modeled unconditional acceptance. A client may tell himself or herself, "My therapist likes me and accepts me, so this shows I am a good and worthy person." Ellis made a case that this is *conditional* self-acceptance. He maintained that such undue warmth "may lead to the entrenchment of clients' needs for love and approval" (Dryden & Ellis, 2001, p. 316). More is said on this topic in the next chapter when the "how to do this" is addressed.

Equally challenging is UOA. Through REBT/CBT, a person is encouraged to realize that no matter how abominable another person's actions may be, it is the action that is to be condemned, not the person. Recall the 2006 tragedy in the one-room Amish schoolhouse when 11 young children were shot and five of them died. The grandfather of one of the girls who was killed remarked, "We must not think evil of this man." Ellis would call this UOA. In Christian terms, love the sinner but not the sin.

Likewise, ULA can be demanding. The REBT/CBT counselor encourages his or her client to recognize that life may bring horrific tragedies. The Holocaust was real. The events of September 11, 2001, are still emblazoned in our memories. Hurricane Sandy devastated much of the New York and New Jersey shores in 2012 at the cost of nearly 66 billion dollars. The more recent shooting of 27 people, including 20 children, in Newtown, Connecticut, in December 2012, is still painfully fresh in our minds. Yes, injustices do occur and should be addressed. They are not dismissed or minimized. In fact, they should be deplored. But for the REBT/CBT counselor, the focus is on helping the client deal with such issues in a way that is not self-defeating. The counselor cares about the client and wants to assure that the client learns healthy ways to cope with whatever may come his or her way.

While Ellis himself (1973) recognized the importance of such skills as a reflection of feelings and empathetic listening in facilitating progress in the REBT/CBT approach to therapy, he himself was intentionally cautious so as not to equate these with the purpose and the essence of the therapeutic relationship. In his own words:

> I am deliberately not very warm or personal with my clients, even those who crave and ask for such warmth, since I quickly explain to them, their main problem is usually that they think they need to be loved, when they actually do not; and I am here to teach them that they can get along very well in this world *without* necessarily being approved or loved by others. (Ellis, 1973, p. 155)

Ellis (1977b) did recognize that there were REBT/CBT counselors who saw some compatibility between a Rogerian-like warmth in the relationship, however, he again cautioned that this could lead to a kind of dependency. His aim was always to help the client accept her or himself independent of the need for the counselor's approval. Ellis viewed such helping as the primary component in the therapeutic alliance.

Since each client comes to counseling or therapy for reasons and backgrounds that are unique to the individual, it is reasonable to understand that establishing bonds will need to be appropriate to the individual.

Anecdotally, Dryden (1991) recounted how he came to this realization when he was on a sabbatical and working at the Philadelphia Center for Cognitive Therapy in 1981. On one afternoon, he saw two different clients.

The first client was impressed with his British credentials and, in speaking with her, it was clear that her preference was to have a very formal relationship with him. In subsequent sessions, Dryden always wore a suit and tie and referred to himself as Dr. Dryden. Once he inadvertently called her by her first name and she reminded him that she didn't think that such informality was proper protocol. Similarly, when he tried to use a bit of self-disclosure as a therapeutic intervention, she responded quite vehemently, "Young man, I am not paying you good money to hear about your problems" (p. 134).

His second client began the first session by stating that he was changing counselors since he didn't like the formality of his former counselor. As a result, Dryden would remove his suit jacket and tie and he and the client used their first names. Dryden reflected that there must be flexibility when trying to establish the bond.

Garfield (1989; 1995) also reflected on the therapeutic relationship in REBT by listening to tapes of actual therapy sessions done by Ellis himself. He did recognize that common aspects of psychotherapeutic systems were not initially emphasized and the therapeutic relationship in REBT had not received adequate recognition. However, he argued that there are specific features of REBT/CBT that both recognize the value and even foster the therapeutic alliance between the counselor and the client. Consider his observations. I invite you to reflect on five of these with examples I provide.

First, the therapeutic alliance is dyadic and therefore relational. The client must trust that the counselor knows what he or she is doing and the counselor trusts that the client has the potential to change. I concur with Garfield that the trained REBT counselor does give the impression that he or she is competent and such competence may inspire confidence. This is most often done through a Socratic method of questioning when the counselor underscores the causes for emotional disturbance and teaches the client how to challenge his or her disturbed thinking (Becker & Rosenfeld, 1976; Ellis & Grieger, 1977).

Second, the therapeutic bond is strengthened when the counselor *actively* attempts to understand the client and help the client solve his or her problem.

Consider this brief excerpt from a client who was seeing Ellis about her panic over whether a procedure she had devised would work and what her employer might say about it if it failed. This is part of her third session. Ellis (1962) is most definitely active:

> Therapist: Yes, let's get back to the essentials. As I have already explained to
> you . . . you worry only because you tell yourself something just
> before you start worrying, and because that something you tell

yourself is nonsense. Now point one is that you must admit that you *are* telling yourself something to start your worrying going, and you must begin to look, and I mean really *look*, for specific nonsense with which you keep reindoctrinating yourself.

Patient: And that is it?

T: And that is perfectly true followed by a ridiculously false statement. The true statement is: "If my testing procedure doesn't work, and if I keep worrying about things like this as much as I am now doing, I will continue to be unable to concentrate on anything very well during the day, and sooner or later, my co-workers will see that I am becoming woefully inefficient, and they will not want me on the job." Perfectly sane, this sentence; nothing crazy about it at all.

P: And the ridiculously false statement that I am saying to myself?

T: The false statement is: "If, because my testing procedure doesn't work and I am functioning inefficiently on my job, my co-workers do not want me or approve of me, then I shall be a worthless person."

P: But wouldn't I be worthless—good for nothing—if I couldn't work properly on this or any other job and no one wanted to associate with me professionally?

T: No, you would then be handicapped or inconvenienced. But your failure as a professional would have nothing to do with your intrinsic worth, or your value to yourself. (pp. 161–162)[1]

This Socratic interaction in which the counselor actively engages the client to confirm or disconfirm hypothetical questions is built into the training of an REBT/CBT counselor (DiGiuseppe, Leaf, & Linscott, 1993). Garfield (1989; 1995) was correct in noting that REBT/CBT counselors don't simply nod their head and/or use encouragers such as umm hums. They are actively involved.

Third, complimenting the client's competence and ability to change is also relational. Ellis was noted to praise his clients, very often complimenting them on their appearance, intelligence, and ability to improve. Earlier, Becker and Rosenfeld (1976) made this same observation.

Consider these few remarks in the second session to a 23-year-old woman who felt guilty about not wanting to follow the demands of her mother and father in adhering to their strict religious rules:

C: My mother is having a rough time yet, because of having her breast removed. She hardly says anything. She's really in a world of fog. She gets confused, and she uses the confusion to give her a hold on her family. She

---

[1] *Source:* Ellis, A. (1962). *Reason and emotion in psychotherapy: A new and comprehensive method of treating human disturbances.* Secaucus, NJ: Citadel Press.

was putting on a martyr act the other night; and I usually would have given in to her, but I said, "Quit being a martyr! Go to bed." She just looked at me like I was a strange creature!

T: And you didn't get upset by it?

C: No, I didn't get upset by it. I had the feeling that I was doing the right thing. And that was, I think, a major accomplishment in the past few days.

T: Yes; that was quite a good accomplishment.

C: Now if there are bigger crises that will come, I don't know how I'll face them; but it looks like I can.

T: Yes, and if you keep facing these smaller crises as they arise—and they tend to be continual—there's no reason why you shouldn't be able to face the bigger ones as well. Why not?

C: I guess it's a case of getting into a good habit.

T: Yes, that's right: getting ready to believe that no matter what your parents do, no matter how hurt they get, that's not your basic problem. You're not deliberately doing them in; you're just standing up for yourself. (Ellis, 1971a, pp. 242–243)

Fourth, pointing out and challenging clients to examine their irrational thoughts or cognitive distortions is a demonstration that the counselors actually do care.

Consider an intervention with a family member who may have a serious drug or alcohol addiction problem. According to the Center for Addiction recovery, the intervention is a "loving process into a troubled person's life" (http://www.center-for-addiction-recovery.com). I argue the same is true for the challenges presented by practitioners of REBT/CBT. While Ellis's style may have appeared gruff when he was engaging a client, he never attacked the person, only the person's irrational beliefs. He never called a person "nutty," only the person's beliefs.

Finally, a completed homework assignment suggests a trust between the client and counselor and therefore helps in building the therapeutic alliance. Homework assignments are integral to REBT/CBT. These assignments help the client understand his or her concerns and also may serve as a guide for the counselor when the client is not in session (Dattilio, 2002). More detailed descriptions of some of the homework assignments are discussed in Chapter 3. Consider this brief example of homework given by Ellis (1962) in a session with a man who had recently played golf with a group of unfriendly men:

[Client] C: What shall I do then?

[Therapist] T: I'll tell you exactly what to do. I want you to play golf, if you can, with those same men again. But this time, instead of trying

	to get them to love you or think you're a grand guy or anything like that, I want you to do one simple thing.
C:	What is that?
T:	I want you merely to *observe*, when you're with them and they don't love you, to observe what you say to you. That's all. Do you think you can do that?
C:	I don't see why not. Just watch my own sentences, what I say to me?
T:	Yes, just that. (p. 125)[2]

In addition to Garfield's (1989; 1995) reflections, I also suggest that interest in the client's current and meaningful challenges builds a therapeutic relationship. Putting the client's actual concerns rather than hypothesizing about some underlying origin or function of the problem actually puts the client relationship front and center. Such focus on the here and now without denying the past, hypothesizing, confronting, and the active interviewing style of the counselor are viewed by DiGiuseppe (1991) as the building blocks of the therapeutic alliance. He believes these are ways of letting clients know that the counselor is trying to understand them, help them solve their problems, and collaborate with them on accepting or refuting the initial hypothesis of the counselor.

Albeit not warm and fuzzy, as mentioned above, REBT/CBT practitioners do recognize the therapeutic value of using humor in psychotherapy as a means of enhancing the therapeutic alliance. Ellis (1977a) explained that his brand of humor "consists of practically every kind of drollery ever invented—such as taking things to an extreme, reducing ideas to absurdity, puns, witticisms, evocative language, paradoxical intentions, slang, [and] deliberate use of sprightly obscenity" (p. 264). In an effort to help clients recognize and attack the irrationality of perfectionism, he would refer to people as FFHs "fallible fucked-up humans" (Ellis, 1977, p. 266). It is important for prospective counselors to keep in mind that such humorous interventions, however, were used with an intention of helping the client learn to develop USA.

Sultanoff (1992) also believed that such humor can bring people together and, in the context of therapy, create a base that facilitates growth. His belief is that "we are going to eventually discover that the most dramatic health benefits of humor are not in the laughter, but in the cognitive and emotional management that humorous experiences provide. The experience of humor relieves emotional distress and assists in changing negative thinking patterns" (Sultanoff, 1992, p. 1). Although slightly cautious about

---

[2] *Source*: Ellis, A. (1962). *Reason and emotion in psychotherapy: A new and comprehensive method of treating human disturbances.* Secaucus, NJ: Citadel Press.

using humor in therapy, Richman (1996) concluded that when used appropriately it has the potential of drawing the client and counselor together and can "even save lives" (p. 560). Moreover, Nelson (2007) suggested that in psychotherapy research, the focus is too often on the laughter that is elicited by humor. She would rather have counselors more explicitly view laughter as an attachment behavior within the therapeutic relationship. Goldin and Bordan (1999) also highlighted how humor may strengthen the therapeutic alliance. Following is one of their vignettes, which magnifies irrational beliefs to absurdity.

Ms. A was a 43-year-old divorced, unemployed mother of two preteens, who sought counseling because of depression and substance abuse issues. She was particularly inclined to blame herself for all of her family's and extended family's problems. She had grown up in an alcoholic environment and found it difficult to find any humor in life's foibles and events. At a specific time in the counseling session, the counselor used humor to aid her in appreciating that not all occurrences could be linked in a cause-and-effect way to her. The interaction was as follows.

Ms. A: My children are experiencing all kinds of school problems. The school is thinking of holding my younger son back. I don't know what to do. I am sure that it has to do with me. I have made it difficult for my son to do anything.

Counselor: You have made it difficult for your sons to do all things—personal and academic.

Ms. A: Yes, that's right. They are nervous because I am nervous and I have caused them to not even be able to do their homework.

Counselor: Let me try to understand this. You have caused them to be unable to do their homework. Have you broken their arms, not paid the electricity bills, or played loud music in order to distract them?

Ms. A: [Taking the question seriously and without any humor implicit in her response] No—I haven't done that.

Counselor: Well, could you help me to understand exactly what you did or do to prevent them from completing their assignments?

Ms. A: Well, it's nothing specific. They are probably just unhappy to have me as a mother, worried about my relationships. You know—whatever. They are not the only ones. My whole family probably blames me for everything. It's my fault that my brothers don't talk to each other and that my mother is sick right now.

Counselor: Have you been watching television lately? The president just went on TV to discuss the economy. I should think that he would have mentioned you directly.

Ms. A: What do you mean by that?

Counselor: Well, it seems to me that you blame yourself, hold yourself account-
able for everything. Have you considered attributing any inflation
worries or depressed economy or global warming or increased
terrorist activities all to you? I am surprised that you left those
out. [Author's Note. The counselor used this particular humorous
intervention only after establishing a strong "working relationship"
with this client.]

Ms. A: [For the first time appreciating the humor in the question—she
began to laugh and her facial expression freed up] I guess you are
right. I do tend to blame myself for everything. [She continued to
laugh] (p. 408)[3]

The above dialogue demonstrates how humor enabled the client to
challenge her negative thoughts, and she subsequently referred to this as a
"world economy joke" (Goldin & Bordan, p. 408).

Components of the Alliance in REBT/CBT

In practical terms, how does the REBT/CBT counselor establish this therapeutic alliance? DiGiuseppe (1991) pointed out that in many mental health
settings a formalized intake assessment often takes place. A client may be
asked to fill out a lengthy psychosocial history with information that may
or may not be relevant to the client. If it is not relevant to the client, this will
be a distraction from establishing the alliance. Also, underlying this seems
to be the assumption that the client is willing to admit in this initial interview to his or her shameful emotions and struggles. DiGiuseppe maintained
that this is often counterproductive and a client, in the first session, is likely
to withhold his or her innermost thoughts and feelings. Ellis and Grieger
(1977) maintained that for REBT/CBT counselors, the principle way to
establish the therapeutic alliance is to help the client find a solution to his
or her immediate presenting concern. DiGiuseppe (1991) suggests that the
alliance develops when the counselor asks the client to identify the current
concern. After listening to the client, the counselor helps the client identify
the client's rational and/or irrational beliefs.

One specific way to foster the treatment alliance has been put forth by
Grosse Holtforth and Castonguay (2005). They argued that the "one-size-fits-
all" notion of interventions may prove unproductive. They proposed that

[3] *Source:* Goldin, E., & Bordan, T. (1999). The use of humor in counseling: The laughing
cure. *Journal of Counseling & Development, 77,* 405–410: JCD by American Counseling
Association. Reproduced with permission of American Counseling Association in the format
Republish in a book via Copyright Clearance Center.

alliance fostering in REBT/CBT "should be customized to the client's motivational goals on order to provide the client with need satisfying experiences" (Grosse Holtforth & Castonguay, 2005, p. 445). What motivates the client to satisfy his or her needs or what does the client avoid so that his or her needs are not frustrated? By assessing the answer to these questions, the counselor is encouraged to provide *need-satisfying experiences* to match these goals. They suggested that this *motivational attunement* with a client is a way of fostering each of the components of the therapeutic alliance proposed by of Bordin (1979) namely, *bond*, *tasks*, and *goals*. Following are examples of how this could be done.

Bond

A client comes to therapy after learning that his wife has been diagnosed with Alzheimer's disease. They have no children, and he is feeling conflicted about assuming the role of caretaker. He is used to spending every Saturday with his buddies golfing. He loves his wife yet feels guilty that he would rather be out on the golf course. The counselor might respond empathetically: "Because you have a very strong need for more personal freedom, this must be very difficult for you." Such motivational attunement may assist in conveying to the client that the counselor is being empathetic and will strengthen their bond.

Goals

A client comes to therapy because she was recently in a car accident and is afraid to drive. She has panic attacks when she thinks of getting behind the wheel again. Her husband works during the day. They have a son who recently joined a soccer league. She loves to be supportive of him. A motivationally attuned treatment goal for her might be this: "I will be able to get my son to practice and enjoy seeing him on the field." Motivationally attuned treatment goals will be more appealing to the client if the amelioration of the presenting problem is matched with an approach goal that is appealing to the client.

Tasks

A client comes to therapy because his parents insist that he attends a college that is nearby so that he can stay at home and commute. He wants to attend a college that is out of state where he can board. There are no financial constraints, and he feels that he wants more independence.

While he is still negotiating with his parents, the counselor might explore motivationally attuned tasks that allow this client to look into activities that get him away from home for shorter periods of time. Perhaps after graduation he and his friends can rent an apartment at the shore for the summer.

Moreover, the three components mutually support one another, since motivationally attuned goals and tasks promote bonding. This reciprocity is also supported by Wright and Davis's (1994) assertion that the "therapeutic relationship is an essential, interactive component of cognitive-behavioral therapy" (p. 42). Theses authors attempted to discover what clients' expectations were. From interviews and videotapes of clients in an outpatient clinic, they drew up a hypothetical letter that a client might address to a counselor. The following suggestions are condensed from that letter:

- First, provide a safe and professional setting for our meeting.
- Second, treat me with respect as a person.
- Third, take my concerns seriously.
- Fourth, I want to think you have my best interests in mind.
- Fifth, I want you to know what you are doing.
- Sixth, give me practical information.
- Seventh, allow me to make choices with your information and suggestions.
- Eighth, stay flexible in your thinking about me.
- Ninth, follow up on your recommendations.
- Tenth, pace yourself. If you are overworked, unhappy, or tense, I may think you aren't being a very good example. (Wright & Davis, 1994, pp. 30–34)

A more research-based approach was taken by Rector, Zuroff, and Segal (1999), who were interested in exploring the interaction between the technical aspects of cognitive behavioral therapy and the nontechnical or common factors involved in the therapeutic alliance. Clients who were diagnosed with depression received individualized cognitive behavioral therapy. These authors found that there was a significant correlation between pretreatment depressive beliefs and the ability to form an alliance. Second, they found a significant correlation between a client's agreement with the goals and tasks in treatment and a lessening of depressive beliefs. Third, they found an interaction between the bond scores and the change in depressive belief scores. The better the therapeutic bond scores in clients who reported fewer depressive beliefs, the greater the outcome in therapy. The authors posited, "A common misperception is that the quality of the alliance in CT is important, but not pivotal" (p. 321).

Stages in Developing the Alliance

The therapeutic alliance is pivotal in REBT/CBT. However, integrating the components takes place over time. Hardy, Cahill, and Barkham (2007) examined 112 review articles pertaining to the therapeutic relationship. From this review they mapped out a model of the stages of relationship building: (a) establishing a relationship, (b) developing a relationship, and (c) maintaining a relationship (p. 27). Each stage has specific objectives.

Establishing the Relationship

In the early stages of therapy, Hardy et al. (2007) described four objectives: (1) expectations, (2) intentions, (3) motivation, and (4) hope. They noted the importance of building positive expectations in the client regarding what should be expected on the part of both the client and counselor. During this early stage, the counselor will need to discover what the client's intentions are and how motivated he or she is to change. At this beginning stage, it is important for the counselor to instill in the client a sense of hope that change is possible. This is very much in line with Bordin's (1979) notion of the need to develop an agreement between the counselor and the client on the *tasks* and goals of therapy.

Developing the Relationship

During this second phase, Hardy et al. (2007) described three objectives: (1) helping the client be open to the process of therapy, (2) helping the client develop a sense of trust in the counselor, and (3) helping the client make a commitment to the process of therapy with the counselor. They suggested that psychodynamic therapies are more likely to engage in exploring dynamics of transference and countertransference at this stage. However, cognitive behavioral counselors are more likely to give feedback messages that have the potential to promote change on the part of the client. This aspect is also discussed in detail in the following chapter.

Maintaining the Relationship

During this stage in therapy, the objectives focus on (a) maintaining satisfaction on the part of the client, (b) maintaining the positive alliance, (c) allowing the client to express her or his emotions, and (d) allowing the client to experience a changing view of herself or himself. Again, similar to Bordin's (1979) notion of the *bond*, Hardy et al. (2007) reached the same conclusion. Regardless of the specific aspects that may be emphasized in different therapeutic schools, it is the quality and strength of the relationship between the client and counselor that is of the utmost importance.

As future counselors, I invite you to reflect on the above. How will you interact with your future clients to build that positive therapeutic relationship?

Assessing the Therapeutic Alliance in REBT/CBT

While historically the concept of the therapeutic alliance had its origin in psychoanalytic literature (Bordin, 1979), this original notion could not be tested in any systematic scientific fashion (Horvath, 2005). Skinner (1985) and the behaviorists did accept the challenge to observe behavior in a more objective manner, yet they contended that only observable behaviors should be the subject of investigation and that these behaviors could change and be shaped through conditioning. In psychotherapy, the therapeutic alliance was not initially observable. But with technological advances, in the middle of the 20th century, therapy sessions could be recorded and observed. This opened the possibility of analyzing the therapeutic alliance in a more systematic way (Horvath, 2005). While the following list is not exhaustive, four of the most commonly used instruments to measure the therapeutic alliance in REBT/CBT are detailed.

Barrett-Lennard Inventory

One of the earliest measures of the therapeutic relationship was developed by Barrett-Lennard (1962). This original version, the Barrett-Lennard Inventory (BLI), was a 92-item, six-point Likert-like scale in which the client rates the counselor. It was based on Rogerian concepts and contained five scales: (1) empathetic understanding, (2) congruence, (3) level of regard, (4) unconditionality of regard, and (5) willingness to be known. Over the years, it has been used in many studies in different contexts (Kurtz & Grummon, 1972; Mills & Zytowski, 1967).

Penn Helping Alliance Scales

Another early measure of the therapeutic alliance was a set of scales that were developed at the University of Pennsylvania (Luborsky, Crits-Christoph, Alexander, Margolis, & Cohen, 1983). These Penn Scales were based on two psychodynamic conceptualizations of the alliance. The first type of alliance, typical in the earlier stages of therapy, indicated that the client held the perception that the counselor would be supportive and able to help. The second type of alliance indicated a view that therapy was more of a collaboration between the counselor and the client. These initial scales required observers to rate transcripts or videos of the sessions. Later, these scales were adapted into a self-report measure from the perspective of both the client and the counselor.

Working Alliance Inventor

However, as I mentioned above, the relationship is more than the bond. One of the seminal assessment instruments that built on Bordin's tripartite (*bond, tasks, goals*) understanding of the therapeutic alliance is the Working Alliance Inventory (WAI) (Horvath & Greenberg, 1989). The WAI is a 36-item rating scale with 12 items on each of the three subscales. Each item is rated on a Likert-like scale that ranges from 1 to 7, beginning with 1, indicating that a good alliance is never present, through 7, indicating that a good alliance is always present. There is a client version, a counselor version, and an observer version. It is considered pantheoretical in the sense that it is not based on one particular definition of the alliance.

California Psychotherapy Alliance Scale

The California Psychotherapy Alliance Scale (CALPAS) was developed by Marmar, Weiss, and Gaston (1989). This scale contains 24 items that tap into four dimensions of the alliance: (1) a measure of the ability of the client to work purposely in therapy, (2) a measure of the attachment bond between the client and the counselor, (3) a measure of the counselor's empathy and emotional engagement, and (4) a measure of the agreement between the counselor and the client regarding the goals of therapy.

Research Supporting the Alliance in REBT/CBT

While there may have been a tendency in the early development of REBT/CBT to view the alliance as necessary but not absolutely essential in promoting change (Lazarus, 1989), there is growing recognition that the alliance is at the heart of treatment and must not be overshadowed by specific techniques. It is the most robust predictor of progress in therapy (Duncan, 2002b; Lambert & Barley, 2001; Martin et al., 2000). This is evident in a growing body of research that incorporates measures of the therapeutic alliance as a significant variable. This is true for REBT/CBT. I review a sample of these studies to demonstrate that more and more REBT/CBT counselors are putting the therapeutic alliance front and center.

Although the Barrett-Lennard Relationship Inventory (BLRI) has its roots in the Rogerian notions of unconditional positive regard, empathy, and congruence, it has also been used in conjunction with the WAI (Salvio, Beutler, Wood, & Engle, 1992). These authors relied on both WAI and the BLRI. They compared the strength of the alliance in focused-expressive psychotherapy, cognitive therapy, and supportive/self-directed therapy in clients being treated for depression. While they found no significant differences between the three types of psychotherapy, they concluded that in all treatments the strength of the alliance early in therapy was the best predictor of the strength at the termination of therapy. It was *the common factor*!

Somewhat more ambiguous were the conclusions of Beckham (1989). With the clients whose depression scores indicated improvement, Beckham surmised that it may have been due to the strong BLI therapeutic alliance or possibly that improvement had begun prior to treatment and these clients were continuing to improve. In either case, the alliance measure was considered important enough to include it as a variable.

On the other hand, Raue, Goldfried, and Barkham (1997), using only the WAI, measured the strength of the alliance between psychodynamic-interpersonal therapy and cognitive behavioral therapy in clients diagnosed with depression. Those clients receiving CBT rated their counselors with significantly higher alliance scores. The alliance is important!

Similarly, Castonguay, Goldfried, Wiser, Raue, and Hayes (1996) found that there was a significant positive relationship between the alliance scores as measured by the WAI and the improvement of depressive symptoms in patients who were receiving cognitive therapy for depression with or without medication. These authors emphasized the importance of the therapeutic alliance as an instrument of change. Again, it is a common factor!

Moreover, Winter and Watson (1999) compared alliance differences between personal construct counselors and cognitive behavioral counselors. Using the BLI as one measure of the relationship, these authors hypothesized that personal construct counselors would be rated as higher on all scales. They did receive higher scores on the unconditionality scale, but, contrary to prediction, the cognitive-behavioral counselors received significantly higher empathy scores. Clients did perceive cognitive behavioral counselors as offering Rogerian-like conditions. Cognitive behavioral counselors don't overlook the alliance!

Stiles, Agnew-Davis, Hardy, Barkham, and Shapiro (1998) also compared the alliance differences over the course of treatment between clients receiving either cognitive behavioral or psychodynamic-interpersonal therapy for treatment of depression. They developed a five-factor scale to measure the strength of the alliance, the Agnew Relationship Measure (ARM). They found positive correlations between the alliance measures and treatments in both treatment groups across all five scales, suggesting the relationship as a common factor. Interestingly, the counselors in the CBT group were rated significantly higher by client ratings on the Partnership and Confidence subscales. Again, the alliance was a common factor and the CBT counselors fared well!

Again, although Watson and Geller (2005) hypothesized that clients receiving process-experiential therapy (PET) for depression would rate their counselors higher on the WAI scale and a Relationship Inventory, compared to clients receiving CBT, their results did not support their prediction. While the clients receiving PET reported feeling more highly regarded by their counselors, there were no significant differences in the clients' ratings of empathy, acceptance, and congruence. Both treatments were effective in treating depression. And again, the therapeutic alliance was the common factor!

Muran et al. (1995) looked specifically at the therapeutic alliance in a cognitive behavioral treatment for depressed and anxious clients. Using a number of outcome measures, these authors found two variables that were most predictive of improvement in depressive symptoms. These included the strength of the therapeutic relationship as measured by CALPAS and the client-reported cognitive shifts regarding his or her attitudes, beliefs, or expectations.

Interestingly, Hyer and Kramer (2004) discussed the efficacy of cognitive behavioral therapy yet pointed out some of the limitations when it is used with older adults. Rather than focusing on the unique components of CBT, they encouraged counselors to integrate a common-factors approach into CBT so that the therapeutic alliance can be enhanced. They recommended altering CBT so that extra effort and sessions are put into helping the client recognize that his or her challenges can be dealt with. They also suggested that it may be harder for older adults to accept the notion that emotions and behaviors are elicited by a thought process. In other words, helping older adults recognize their dysfunctional thoughts will need extra time and patience on the part of the counselor. Likewise, older adults may be more reluctant to change or have fewer functional skills or resources necessary to make changes. It is a challenge for the counselor to draw on such resources through images or metaphors, even faith-based rituals. Finally, the counselor must remain sensitive to the emotional struggles that an older client may be experiencing in the face of cognitive decline.

Rational Humorous Songs

I bring this chapter to an end by inviting you to sing a tune that reflects one of Ellis's specialties. In concluding remarks about his views on intimacy, relationship, and dependence in psychotherapy, Ellis (1977b) discussed his then relatively new technique of using rational humorous songs. He did this specifically as a way to combine cognition and affect in an attempt to help his clients recognize absurdities and laugh at themselves. He wanted clients to learn the importance of unconditional self-acceptance more than the need to be accepted because the therapist accepts them. Here is one of those songs that pokes fun at the idea that "psychotherapy and all-encompassing love are synonymous" (Ellis, 1977b, p. 18).

"Beautiful Hang-up"
(set to the tune of Stephen Foster's "Beautiful Dreamer")

Beautiful hang-up, why must we part
When we have shared our whole lives from the start?
We are so used to taking course,
Oh, what a crime it would be to divorce!
Beautiful hang-up, don't go away!
Who will befriend me if you do not stay?
Though you will make me look like a jerk,
Living without you would take so much work!
Living without you would take so much work![4]

Note: If you are not familiar with this tune, you can listen to it being sung by Bing Crosby at http://www.youtube.com/watch?v=wtgklHQ52WE.

Summary

- Despite arguments to the contrary, the therapeutic relationship is the quintessential common factor in REBT/CBT. Both Ellis and Beck developed their respective approaches to therapy because they paid attention to their clients' needs. However, the relationship is expressed in different ways.
- In REBT/CBT the therapeutic relationship is a collaborative partnership. It is established between the counselor and the client by agreeing on three essential components of therapy: (1) the bond, (2) the goals of therapy, and (3) the completion of "homework" tasks involved.
- *Unconditional self-acceptance* is fostered, and this is not based solely on the fact that the counselor has assumed a nonjudgmental stance toward the client.
- Empirical evidence has supported that in REBT/CBT the therapeutic relationship is a threefold process: (1) establishing the relationship, (2) developing the relationship, and (3) maintaining the relationship.
- A number of validated scales have been used to assess the effectiveness of the therapeutic relationship in REBT/CBT.

---

[4] *Source:* Ellis, A. (Speaker). (1971c). A garland of rational humorous songs [Cassette recording]. New York: Institute for Rational-Emotive Therapy. Printed with permission.

2

Basic Tenets of REBT/CBT

While there have been some arguments against applying the concept of placebo to psychotherapy (Herbert & Gaudiano, 2005; Kirsch, 2005; Lambert, 2005), Lambert concluded that it would be better to focus on such causal mechanisms as expectation for improvement as a common factor. But how does REBT/CBT purport to enhance the client's expectations that she or he might be able to make changes? I argue that for the REBT/CBT counselor, it is part and parcel of the approach. This chapter focuses on some of the specific aspects of REBT/CBT that enhance expectations as well as promote the therapeutic alliance.

Generally, REBT and broad-based CBT may be considered synonymous, although there are some initial differences that might be considered. Ellis's (1993) primary emphasis was somewhat more philosophically based, while Beck was initially focused on searching for empirical evidence for a theory of depression (Alford & Beck, 1997; Beck & Alford, 2009; Beck, Rush, Shaw, & Emery, 1979; Padesky & Beck, 2003; Rush & Beck, 1978). Ellis subsequently made some distinctions in what he called *specialized* or *preferential* REBT versus CBT.

Still, and interestingly, both Albert Ellis and Aaron Beck were trained in psychoanalysis and began their careers as psychoanalysts. These two giants independently began to question the efficacy of psychoanalysis and turned instead to examining the role of cognitive processes in emotional disturbances. While their origins are distinct, there is a fundamental agreement between REBT and CBT that (a) our cognitions may affect our behavior, (b) our cognitions may be changed, and (c) our behaviors and emotions may change as a result of our changes in cognitions. In this chapter I provide a description of the basic tenets of REBT and CBT suggesting similarities and differences and show how this approach to psychotherapy has been demonstrably effective.

REBT in a Nutshell

Philosophically, Ellis was strongly influenced by the writings of Stoic philosophers such as Epictetus and Marcus Aurelius (Dryden & Ellis, 2001; Ellis, 1977b, 2007; Ellis & Grieger, 1977). He has often been noted to quote Epictetus: "People are disturbed not by things but by their view of things." In other words, "It is not the things themselves that worry us, but the opinions that we have about those things" (Wessler & Wessler, 1980, p. 238).

Likewise, Ellis (1977b) elaborated on the importance of self-acceptance and clearly distinguished self-acceptance from self-evaluation. In making this distinction, Ellis (1977b) also made direct reference to the work of philosopher Bertrand Russell, who espoused that self-centered passions including self-pity and self-admiration shut one's self in a personal prison. Wessler and Wessler (1980) characterized REBT as the "applied philosophy of Russell" (p. 3).

Although Ellis was familiar with the work of Alfred Adler, it was not until Ellis gave his first public paper on rational-emotive therapy in 1956 that others pointed out to him the significant overlap in the two approaches (Ellis, 1962). Adler emphasized the importance of life's goals and Ellis (1962) explained that, similar to his own emphasis on beliefs and attitudes, life's goals are a form of thought. Ellis (1962) also noted that Adlerians tried to help individuals learn that inferiority resulted from self-devaluation, similar to REBT counselors who explain inadequacy in terms of irrational self-beliefs.

Emotional Disturbance

Ellis (1993) proposed a biopsychosocial explanation of human emotions. He posited that humans are born with a tendency toward growth and also learn goals and preferences from environmental influences including family and society. Ellis (1962) proposed that individuals are propagandized by parents and society to hold certain values such as the need to be loved but then "repropagandize" (p. 191) themselves to blindly accept these notions. He described this as a "triple-headed propagandistic broadside" (p. 192).

Foremost in Ellis's theory, however, is the role of cognitions in the influence on emotions and behaviors (Ellis, 1962, 1971a, 1977a, 1989b, 2004).

He recognized that humans have an innate tendency to mentally construct absolute demands about their goals and preferences. He described these demands as self-defeating and irrational. Emotional disturbance comes about by irrational beliefs about one's goals and preferences.

ABCs of REBT

In training future counselors, I often begin by asking students the question: "What pushes your buttons?" There have been a wide variety of answers: "driving behind a slow driver on a main highway," "pop quizzes," "rude people," "waiting in line." I then proceed to explain that the students really push their own buttons. Ask yourself this question and keep your answer in mind.

As a prospective counselor, to introduce you to the tenets of REBT, I invite you to reflect on this scenario. Close your eyes and imagine yourself alone in New York City. This is your very first visit to New York. You need to travel on the subway to meet your friend. You have never been on the subway system. It is 10:30 at night, and you are supposed to travel to the SoHo district (South of Houston) from Penn Station. You are alone and on the subway platform. You are a bit nervous to begin with. Your friends have advised against this trip. There have been recent reports of women being raped and/or robbed on the subway. Suddenly you feel something like an elbow punch to your rib cage. It hurts and you begin to lose your balance. How are you feeling? What are your emotions? What is your reaction? On a scale of 1 to 10 (1 being very comfortable, 10 being extremely upset) where are you emotionally? Scared? Angry? Frustrated? Open your eyes and write the number down. (I have used this in class and many students expressed a variety of emotions including extreme fear and anger.)

Close your eyes again. Get back to the subway platform. You experience the pain of having your ribs being elbowed. You look around. You notice that there is a man standing next to you with a cane. He is blind. He inadvertently bumped against you. What are your emotions? What is your reaction? Is it the same?

Note that the event itself had not changed. You were still on the subway platform. You still received the elbow to your rib cage. What was different?

With his philosophical understanding that it is not so much the uninvited life events that cause a person to become disturbed, Ellis developed the ABCs of REBT. REBT proposes that people have basic goals such as striving for happiness, self-actualization, and desires for happiness, comfort, and approval. At times, something happens that interferes with achieving these goals. Ellis defined this as an *Activating Event* or

Adversity (A). This activating event is any experience or event that may occur on a daily basis such as failure or rejection (Ellis, 1977b, 2007; Ellis & Lange, 1994).

Ellis (1977b) would explain, for example, that a person might lose her or his job (A). Suppose that this person moped around the house for weeks instead of trying to get another job. This person might say she or he is depressed due to losing the job. The depression and inertia are emotional and behavioral *Consequences* (C).

Ellis would argue that the depression is not the direct result of the lost job. A does not cause C. Rather, Ellis would argue that it is the individual's *Beliefs* about the event (B) that cause the disturbance. An individual might feel disappointed or regretful (C) about losing a job (A) if her or his belief was one of wishing that she or he had not been fired but basically evaluating the job loss as unfortunate or sad. This disappointment is not a disturbed emotion. The person may tell herself or himself that she or he still has ways to enjoy life. However, regret does not make one's self miserable. On the other hand, when the individual believes and internally demands that she or he MUST have the job or judges herself or himself as worthless because he or she can't get meaningful employment and must rely on unemployment (B), these beliefs are characterized as demanding and self-defeating, or irrational. Would losing a job make you feel utterly devastated? Would it outright destroy you?

From the REBT perspective, emotions are not neatly categorized as positive or negative. Rather, they are seen on a continuum. Experiencing sadness (C) when I lose a job (A) or grief (C) when my spouse dies (A) are healthy emotions. Emotions become disturbed when they result from disturbed thinking (Ellis, 1962).

Ellis (1977b) distinguished rational beliefs (rBs) from irrational beliefs (iBs). If a belief is rational (rB), it will be based on objective reality and lead to individual happiness and survival (Ellis, 2007; Wessler & Wessler, 1980). A rational belief is based on notions such as preferences or wishes, and, when the preference is thwarted, a person may become frustrated or disappointed. On the other hand, an underlying an irrational belief is a faulty *appraisal*. It is based on notions of dogmatic absolutistic demands and musts. When thwarted, a person may become damning of oneself or others. Ellis (2007) referred to this as "I-can't-stand-it-itis" (p. 303). A client comes into therapy emotionally upset and proclaims, "My father does not love me." This statement may or may not be true. The primary focus of REBT is not on the veracity of a particular statement but on how the statement is appraised. Irrational beliefs lead to self-defeating and self-destructive consequences (Ellis, 1977b). This would be rational to believe: "It would be preferable for my father to love me." However, this would be irrational to believe: "My father MUST love me." Irrational beliefs are marked by a combination of *awfulizing, demandingness*, and evaluation of one's self or others (Wessler & Wessler, 1980). Ellis has categorized the core iBs of REBT in a number of listings (Ellis & Grieger, 1977; Ellis & Harper, 1975; Ellis & Lange, 1994).

1. You MUST have love and approval by all of the significant people in your life.

2. You MUST NOT fail. You MUST be thoroughly competent, adequate, and achieving if you are to be considered worthwhile.

3. People MUST NOT act in a bad, wicked, or villainous way, and if they do they MUST be blamed or damned and considered as bad and/or villainous people.

4. If you are treated unfairly and things do not go the way you want them to be, it MUST awful and catastrophic.

5. Since you have little or no ability to control your happiness, you MUST be seriously disturbed and miserable when you experience externally caused disturbances or events that are difficult.

6. There MUST be a perfect solution to every problem, and I MUST be able to find it.

7. If something is or may be dangerous or fearsome, you MUST obsess about it and frantically look for ways to avoid even the possibility of it occurring.

8. You MUST be able to avoid certain difficulties and responsibilities and still have a fulfilling life.

9. You MUST have something or someone stronger or greater than yourself to rely on.

10. Because something terrible happened in your past, these past experiences MUST be all important determiners of your present behavior and feelings.

11. You MUST be able to achieve human happiness even if you don't do anything.

12. You MUST be able to be disturbed and upset by others' problems and disturbances since you don't have control over your emotions.

These iBs have been subsumed into three *musturbatory* notions:

1. I absolutely must do well and win the approval of my significant others or else rate myself as worthless or rotten.

2. Significant others must absolutely treat me kindly and fairly in the exact way that I want them to treat me or else they need to be blamed or damned for their inconsiderateness.

3. The conditions under which I live in this world must be arranged in such a way that I can get almost everything that I want quickly and easily and must not get anything that I do not want. (Ellis, 1977b; Ellis & Grieger, 1977)

The D-Es in REBT

The challenge for the REBT counselor is to help the client detect her or his iBs and learn techniques to *Dispute* them (D) (Ellis, 1971a, 1977b, 2004). Often disputation is done through debating. Take the above client who is angry and upset because his father doesn't love him. An *inelegant* solution would be to dispute by using some kind of reframing. Perhaps the father is overwhelmed by his job and feeling financial burdens. Maybe the house is in foreclosure. A more elegant solution is to help the client discover his irrational beliefs and dispute them through Socratic questioning. Where is the evidence that all fathers must love their children? Is there evidence that some fathers do not? A client is also taught to discriminate between wants and needs and desires and demands. A client is helped to see that it is desirable for her or his father to love her or him but demanding the love is self-defeating. Ellis (1977b) explained that after this process of disputation, a client might be led to surrender her or his irrational beliefs and acquire a new *Effect* (E).

Following is an excerpt from a therapy session that Ellis had with a client who had graduated from college, had a good job, and had a steady girlfriend. Still, he had a terrible fear that he might become a homosexual. Ellis (1971a) is disputing and trying to get the client to recognize the difference between preferring and demanding.

T. Now what?

C. I'll always be anxious (*inaudible*).

T. As long as you have necessities, demands, got-to's.

C. (*Inaudible*)

T. Because as soon as you say, "I've *got* to have *x*"—such as be straight—and there's the slightest possibility that you won't, then you'll say "Wouldn't it be *awful* if I were not what I've *got* to be?" While if you're sticking to "It's *desirable* to be straight, but I'm not or might not be," you'll say, "Well, tough shit! So I'd be gay! I wouldn't *like* it. And I'd work against it if I were gay. But what's so goddamned *horrible* about having an undesirable trait?" You see?

C. But that undesirable trait scares me.

T. No! "I scare me, with me got-to's! It isn't the undesirable trait that scares me. Since I *must* be straight, then the mere thought of being gay scares me. But if I *want* to be straight, and right now I'm not, I'd be *concerned* but not *scared*." Do you see the difference? (pp. 112–113)

However, besides the Socratic questioning, there are other techniques that are used to dispute iBs.

Techniques of REBT

While practitioners of REBT might employ a number of cognitive techniques, each is built on the fundamental goal of having a client recognize the need for unconditional self-acceptance (USA). As mentioned in the chapter before, the counselor likewise gives the client unconditional acceptance, though the counselor may be most interactive and challenging. Included below are some of the more common techniques used in REBT. Later in this chapter you will see that many of the practices of CBT are very similar.

Psychoeducational Emphasis. One of the most significant elements that distinguishes REBT is its emphasis on instructing the clients on the basic philosophy and tenets of REBT (Ellis, 1993). Clients are taught that change can happen and should be expected. In the initial sessions in REBT, the counselor specifically teaches a client the relationship between her or his emotional disturbance and the underlying thinking. The client is then taught to dispute the irrational beliefs. Ellis clearly believed that psychotherapy should focus much more on living a happy and self-fulfilled life. He stressed that it was crucial to "teach their clients how to choose more functional solutions to their lives" (Ellis, 2002).

In addition to teaching the basic A-B-C-D-Es of REBT, counselors often use other educational materials. These might include bibliotherapy and/or audiotherapy. Clients are taught problem-solving skills and are invited to attend workshops and lectures.

Ellis was known for his famous free Friday night demonstrations at the Albert Ellis Institute in New York. I recall my last visit to the Institute with a colleague prior to Ellis's death. We witnessed how this 90-year-old legend was still discussing and disputing iBs. He used rational-emotive imagery and invited everyone in the audience to join in singing his rational humorous songs.

Rational-Emotive Imagery. Rational-emotive imagery (REI) was originally developed by Maxie Maultsby and is now one of the main interventions used in REBT (Ellis, 1977a). This technique is designed to help clients learn the rational habits of thinking that are usually the opposite of what they normally experience. An REBT counselor might ask a client to complete an A-B-C-D analysis of the specific event that sparked a disturbing emotional response. For example, a client might come into therapy because of a fear of public speaking. Recently the client was embarrassed because of a blunder that was made when the client gave a report to his coworkers at a regional meeting. His girlfriend was attending the meeting.

The counselor would give a set of instructions to the client to help him or her relax.

1. Take a deep breath. Breathe in and out a slow but continuous motion, take a deep breath and force it out, saying to yourself, "Relax."

2. Now hold your breath for ten seconds, counting "one-thousand one, one-thousand two, one-thousand three," and so on.

3. Do this for a few minutes until you feel relaxed.

After the client is relaxed, he or she is directed to imagine the original disturbing emotion from the A-B-C-D analysis. The client is instructed to picture himself or herself only with the rational thoughts at the D section.

Ellis made some adaptations of REI (Wessler & Wessler, 1980). For example, the client is asked to close his eyes and imagine the presenting situation as exaggeratedly a *worst case scenario*. In the case of the blundering public speaker, coworkers might laugh out loud or even leave the room. The client loses the contract. His girlfriend cancels their dinner date.

As described above, the counselor gives the client sufficient time to get in touch with his feelings. The counselor instructs the client to raise his hand when he is experiencing the emotional distress at point C. The counselor then asks the client to experience his feelings. The client responds that he is feeling awful and depressed and utterly worthless. Next, the counselor asks the client to keep the same image of being in the auditorium making the same blunder but to change his feelings from an unhealthy feeling of awful and depressed and worthless to a healthy negative feeling of "not depressed and worthless, ONLY disappointed" (Ellis, 1977b, p. 202). The client is then asked what he thought about to change the feeling. REI becomes a form of deconditioning in which a client learns rational self-talk.

Shame Attacking Exercises.   In an effort to help a client become more self-accepting and less dependent on the opinion of others, another technique often used in REBT is the *shame attack* (Ellis, 2004). In this exercise a client is invited to do something in public that might appear to be humiliating or even mortifying. Because each client might experience shame or embarrassment in different situations, these exercises are individualized (Wessler & Wessler, 1980). A client is asked what might be shameful or embarrassing. The client is then asked to put himself or herself in that situation. One client might be asked to dress in a silly manner such as a male wearing his tie around his forehead while going into a fancy restaurant. Another client may be asked to loudly call out stops on a bus or subway. These exercises are designed to help the client experience and practice changing her or his beliefs about the emotional consequences of another's perception. The client is asked to report back what she or he said to herself or himself to make the situation bearable.

In an interview with Jeffrey Mishlove, Ellis offered an example that he might suggest such as stopping someone "on the street and say, 'I just got out of the loony bin. What month is it?' and not feel ashamed when they look in horror at you and think you're off your rocker" (Mishlove & Ellis, 1995, p. 45).

I invite you as a prospective counselor to put yourself in a situation that is breaking some socially accepted norm. I have had students do this and report back. One student got into the elevator, faced the rear while everyone else was facing front, and talked out loud. Another example was a student who went into a computer lab class, took off her boots and socks, and walked around the room barefoot. However, I remind you and them not to do anything that might lead to you getting arrested or being fired from a job. The important part of this exercise is to ask yourself, "What did you say to yourself that made the exercise maybe somewhat embarrassing but bearable?"

Humor. As I pointed out in the previous chapter, REBT counselors understand that humor is a way of establishing the therapeutic alliance. It also is a way to help clients dispute their irrational beliefs. Ellis explained that in REBT, counselors use humor intentionally. Ellis (1989b) recalled the example of a woman who came to him with serious suicidal ideation. "Humorously again, I convinced her that even if she killed herself, she would not be a fool or a worm but only a person who was acting foolishly and wormly (that is, against her own interest)" (p. 78). One of her homework assignments was to sing one of his Rational Humorous songs at least three times each day. She left the session laughing and replied to Ellis, "It was a pleasure talking to you" (p. 80).

Ellis explained that "when you're unhumorous, you take things too seriously. . . . We never laugh at you, only the way you think and act and feel, and we show you how to laugh at yourself and not take yourself too seriously, which is what emotional disturbance, again, is" (Mishlove & Ellis, 1995, p. 45).

Ellis's humor can also often be seen in his use of peppery language. He might ask a client something like "Just because you acted in a shitty way, does that make you a shithead?" One of his most recognized coined words is *musterbation*. In REBT, counselors are taught to listen for when a client tells herself or himself that "I must do well," "She must do . . . ," or "The world must. . . ." In principle, if a person doesn't *musterbate*, then she or he wouldn't awfulize and catastrophize and disturb herself or himself. Ellis (1977a) believed that "*musterbation* (is) a form of behavior infinitely more pernicious than masturbation" (p. 263).

Homework. As mentioned in the previous chapter, homework assignments are integral to REBT as well as CBT and the completion of these assignments are indicative that a therapeutic alliance is being built (Garfield, 1989, 1995). But what might be suggested for an REBT assignment? While the assignments might include actual in vivo experiences, such as a person who has a fear of riding elevators might be required to ride an elevator up and down for 10 minutes every day for a week or practicing doing a rational emotive imagery every day for a week, Ellis (1971b) recommended incorporating behavioral self-management procedures into the assignments to help the client condition herself or himself to develop a consistent habit.

For example, after engaging the client in a rational emotive imagery exercise, an REBT counselor might ask a client, "Are you willing to do this every day until we meet for our next session?" After the client agrees, the counselor would add, "What is something that you really dislike doing?" The client might reply, "Dusting the things in my house." The counselor then asks the client, "What is something that you really enjoy doing every day?" The client might reply, "Playing a video game." The counselor then might instruct the client by saying, "Before you play the video game, you will practice this imagery. If you do not practice it, you must dust everything in your house." In his Friday night sessions, Ellis often exaggerated humorously and might have said something like, "And if you don't, you must also go dust everything in your mother's house."

Table 2.1   REBT Summary

A	Activating Event
B	Rational or Irrational Beliefs about the event
C	Emotional or Behavioral Consequence
D	Dispute the Irrational Belief
E	Effect of new Emotion

CBT in a Nutshell

Beck's theory initially focused on experimental testing and clinical observations of persons diagnosed with depression (Alford & Beck, 1997; Beck & Alford, 2009; Beck et al., 1979; Padesky & Beck, 2003; Rush & Beck, 1978). He was originally testing Freud's theory and found it to be lacking. This led to his formulation of what was originally termed the *cognitive theory of depression*.

Basic to Beck's cognitive model are three specific notions: (1) *the cognitive triad*, (2) *schemas*, and (3) *cognitive errors*. There is an underlying assumption that experiences are active processes that lead to *automatic thoughts* that are linked to *schemas* (Beck & Alford, 2009; Rush & Beck, 1978).

Cognitive Triad

According to Beck (1963; 1964), the role of cognitive processing is essential to understanding depression. There are three cognitive patterns that are seen to underlie depression (see Figure 2.1).

The first component centers on how a person views herself or himself. Persons with depression will have a *negative view of themselves*. They will see themselves as worthless, somehow defective and inadequate. They do not believe that they possess the qualities necessary for happiness. Persons who are mildly depressed may report being disappointed in themselves, whereas the more severely depressed might consider themselves despicable and unworthy of living. For example, a person in a situation when a coworker receives recognition for a job well done will automatically think something like "I'm no good" or "I'm a loser" (Beck & Alford, 2009; Rush & Beck, 1978).

The second component involves how a person construes his or her environment. Persons with depression have a *negative view of their experiences in the world*. Their world is devoid of meaning. The environment places too many unreasonable demands on them. Even when evidence is presented that there are alternative interpretations of a situation, depressed persons continue to tailor facts to fit into their negative conclusions. For example, a student who doesn't get the grade he thinks he deserves may

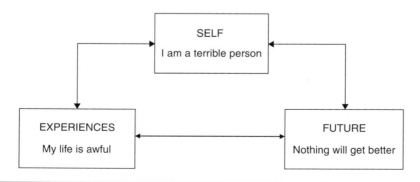

Figure 2.1   Cognitive Triad of Negative Views Leading to Depression

automatically think to himself, "It isn't fair, the teacher plays favorites," even though it was clear that the student didn't follow the rubric that was given.

The third component focuses on how a person views the future. Persons with depression have a *negative view of the future.* They believe that things will never get better. If they have a task to accomplish, they automatically think that it will result in failure. These negative expectations can take the form of fantasies. Even though a person might ordinarily have enjoyed skiing when she was not depressed, she might now fantasize that she probably would fall and break her leg.

With this negative cognitive triad, persons with depression will exhibit certain regressive motivational patterns. There may be a certain *paralysis of the will.* They often are not able to mobilize themselves to perform even the simplest tasks. They may know what they need to do, such as get up and go to work, but often can't do it.

Another motivational pattern that persons with depression often exhibit is *avoidance or escape wishes.* A student may know that a paper is due but can't muster enough energy to do it. In class, that student may daydream rather than pay attention to the professor. A more severely depressed individual might not want to be friends and may even drop out of his or her social circle.

A person with depression will often have *suicidal wishes.* In their research, Beck and Alford (2009) reported that suicidal ideation was reported by 74% of their patients. It took the form of overt expressions such as "I wish I were dead" to more indirect verbalizations like "My family would be better off without me" (pp. 30–31).

These negative self-statements are closely related to Ellis's irrational beliefs—motivations are interdependent and may often lead a person to feelings of dependency and wanting to be helped (Beck & Alford, 2009).

Schemas

A schema is a stable cognitive framework that a person uses to organize and interpret events from a "kaleidoscopic array of stimuli" (Beck, 1964; Rush & Beck 1978). Although different persons may react to situations in different ways, individuals tend to extract aspects that become a coherent pattern that becomes a more or less permanent reaction. While not directly observable, schemas can often be inferred by negative thought patterns. For example, a person may have the schema that he or she must do everything perfectly to avoid being a failure (similar to Ellis's iBs). That person goes to the pool and jumps in for a swim. He or she may begin to think, "I don't swim as well as everyone else."

Cognitive Errors

As a person's depression becomes worse, she or he is less able to see that the schemas are erroneous. This leads to a distortion of the person's thinking. There are a number of cognitive errors in logic that Beck put forth (Beck, 1963; Beck & Alford, 2009; Rush & Beck, 1978).

- *Arbitrary inference* refers to an erroneous conclusion that is made about a situation without supporting evidence or contrary to the evidence that is at hand. There is often an unwillingness to consider alternatives. A person goes into the drug store to get a prescription filled. The druggist isn't smiling. The person may think to himself or herself, "The druggist doesn't care about me." Is there proof? Could the druggist have a headache?
- *Selective abstraction* refers to an erroneous conclusion that is made on the basis of a small detail taken out of context while neglecting the more relevant aspects of the situation. A student may receive a paper with minor corrections on it. The student may say to herself or himself, "The teacher probably thinks that I don't even care about my work."
- *Overgeneralization* refers to an erroneous conclusion based on one single incident. An employee has a project that is due to his boss but he missed the deadline. That employee says to himself, "I'm such a failure, I never do things the way I should."
- *Magnification and minimization* refers to an erroneous conclusion such that negative information is extremely distorted and/or positive information is grossly trivialized. Jim is on a date with his girlfriend. He spills coffee on his shirt. He thinks to himself, "This is a disaster. I'm sure she will never want to see me again." This is magnification. In contrast, Carol's friend's father died and she is at the funeral after baking a cake and taking it to Carol's house. Still, she thinks to herself, "Even this doesn't make up for when I forgot to send her a birthday card last month." This is minimization.
- *Personalization* refers to an erroneous conclusion that a person makes about her or his responsibility for an external event when it is not her or his fault. Dottie's chore is to walk the family dog. When she didn't do it, her mother thought to herself, "I must not be a very good mother since my daughter didn't take her responsibility seriously."

Just as in REBT, the focus of CBT is on helping clients examine their core beliefs and test their accuracy. However, Beck's emphasis is not so much on the *irrationality* of a person's beliefs but rather on the *functionality* of those core beliefs (Padesky & Beck, 2003). Consider the example of a person who holds the belief that "God will protect me." If this belief brings a person spiritual comfort, it would be considered functional. On the other hand, if it leads the person to drive recklessly on the turnpike, it would be quite dysfunctional (Padesky & Beck, 2003). In Beck's cognitive model, *core beliefs* influence a person's attitudes or self-expectations (*intermediate beliefs*), and these give rise to automatic thoughts that influence his or her emotions and behaviors (Beck, 1963).

Techniques in CBT

Similar to REBT, a CBT counselor will question the client, help the client identify illogical thinking patterns, help the client search for alternative solutions, and use many similar cognitive and behavioral interventions. These may include assigning homework, bibliotherapy, using an activity schedule to help the client overcome lack of motivation, cognitive rehearsal, and role playing. Some are more specific to CBT (Beck et al., 1979).

The CBT record is a worksheet to help clients identify automatic and negative thought patterns. Beck et al. (1979) also suggested the use of a modified wrist golf counter as a helpful way for a client become more aware of his or her automatic negative thoughts.

Effectiveness of REBT/CBT

There is sufficient evidence that CBT is an effective treatment for a wide range of conditions (see Hollon & Beck, 1994). While this is not to say that REBT is at all less effective, from its inception, the initial emphasis in CBT was specifically aimed at finding empirical data to support Beck's theory of depression. In comparing CBT and REBT, Padesky and Beck (2003) argued that CBT was more empirically based and REBT was more philosophical. While Ellis (2005) agreed with many of the points that Padesky and Beck made, he disagreed with the criticism that REBT lacked outcome studies. He commented, "Actually, over 200 outcome studies on REBT have been published, but many of them have not been as rigorously done as CT studies" (Ellis, 2005, p. 181).

Depression

Over the years, CBT and psychopharmacology have been called the "gold standard" for the treatment of persons diagnosed with a major depressive disorder (Hollon et al., 2005). CBT has been found to be at least as effective as medication and the effects possibly longer lasting (Hollon & Beck, 1994).

In a meta-analysis review, Dobson (1989) analyzed 28 studies of clients diagnosed with depression who had been treated with (a) CBT, (b) clients who were treated with medications, (c) clients who received behavior or other therapies, and (d) clients who were on the wait list or no treatment control group. Results showed that clients who received CBT showed a greater degree of change.

On the other hand, Siddique, Chung, Brown, and Miranda (2012) found that moderately depressed women who received medication were less depressed after 6 months than those who received CBT, but after 1 year there was no difference. There were no significant differences with women who were severely depressed, but after 1 year those who received CBT were less depressed than those on medication.

Szentagotai, David, Lupu, and Cosman (2008) compared standard CBT, REBT, and medication in the treatment of depression and on changes in thoughts and beliefs. These authors examined the effects of each on measures of (a) irrational beliefs (REBT), (b) intermediate and core beliefs, and (c) automatic thoughts. All three treatments showed changes in the three types of cognitions. In a 6-month follow up, both REBT and CBT participants showed improvement on a measure of depression.

Other Applications

Again, in addition to treating a person with depression, Beck and his colleagues have applied the principles of CBT to a wide scope of disorders (Hollon & Beck, 1994). Books have been published with manuals describing how CBT can be used to treat panic and anxiety disorders (Clark & Beck, 2010) and each of the personality disorders (Beck, Freeman, & Davis, 2004).

Counselors who are interested in working in a school setting will also find REBT/CBT very helpful. Many strategies have also been developed to address the needs of children in the educational setting. Some examples include suggestions for adolescents with eating disorders (Mennuti, Bloomgarden, Mathison, & Gabriel, 2012), developing substance abuse prevention programs in schools (Forman & Sharp, 2012), and implementing bullying prevention interventions (Doll et al., 2012). Interventions for children diagnosed with autism (Bolton, McPoyle-Callahan, & Christner, 2012) and attention deficit hyperactivity disorder are also based on REBT/CBT. Interventions used for the treatment for anxiety are suggested for use with students who are selectively mute (Mulligan & Christner, 2012) and for lesbian, gay, bisexual, transgendered, and questioning (LGBTQ) (Weiler-Timmins, 2012).

Kendall and Hedtke (2006b) developed *The Coping Cat Workbook* for treating anxiety in children. This workbook has been used in the school setting as well in the clinical setting (Gosh, Flannery-Schroeder, & Brecher, 2012).

Common Factors and Challenges of the Medical Model

Focusing on diagnosis might raise a concern from the common factors perspective. Because he contended that psychotherapy is an interpersonal process and not a medical procedure, Elkins (2009) made strong arguments against continuing to use the medical model framework in psychotherapy. I agree that this is a particular challenge for REBT/CBT counselors since there are ample empirically validated studies showing the effectiveness of REBT/CBT.

There has also been concern that overreliance on manualized treatments actually may decrease the therapeutic alliance (Addis, Wade, & Hatgis, 1999). The question then remains: Is the effectiveness of CBT dependent on its use of manualized treatments so results can more easily be controlled?

Beck reminded novice counselors to be wary of "slighting the therapeutic relationship" (Beck et al., 1979). Likewise, even though research supports the effectiveness of both REBT/CBT, Ellis himself never had a manual and would never be constricted to following sessions that might be prescribed. His Friday night sessions were anything but manualized.

Ellis (1989a) himself encouraged variability and commented that "I do . . . considerably vary both my style and content in using RET with radically different clients; and I strongly recommend that other counselors do so" (p. 221). I believe that if REBT/CBT counselors become too wedded to the medical model, Ellis himself might poke fun at this when "presumably intelligent men and women, with hell knows how many academic degrees behind them (which we may unhumorously refer to as degrees of restriction rather than degrees of freedom), consistently take themselves too seriously" (Ellis, 1977a, p. 262).

"Love Me, Love Me, Only Me!"
(To the tune of "Yankee Doodle")

Love me, love me, only me
Or I'll die without you!
Make your love a guarantee,
So I can never doubt you!
Love me, love me, totally
Really, really try dear.
But if you demand love, too,
I'll hate you till I die dear!
Love me, love me all the time,
Thoroughly and wholly!
Life turns into slushy slime
Less you love me soley!
Love me with great tenderness,
With no ifs or buts dear.
If you love me somewhat less,
I'll hate your goddamned guts, dear![1]

---

[1] Ellis, A. (Speaker). (1971c). A garland of rational humorous songs [Cassette recording]. New York: Institute for Rational-Emotive Therapy. Printed with permission.

Summary

- Although REBT developed from a more philosophical stance and CBT from a more empirical base, both agree that cognitions have an effect on emotions.
- Both REBT and CBT have an educational component where clients are specifically taught the basic tenets of each respectively.
- The language of REBT is in the ABCs. The activating event (A) does not cause the emotional consequence (C). Rather, it the irrational beliefs (B) about the event that cause the disturbance. The beliefs that are irrational are disputed (D) through a variety of methods. A new more healthy emotion (E) results.
- CBT uses the language of a *cognitive triad*. A negative view of (a) one's self, (b) of one's world, and (c) one's future underlies the development of depression.
- There are many empirical studies that demonstrate the effectiveness of REBT and CBT.

3

Evolution of REBT/CBT

A t the conclusion of World War II, the Veterans Administration (VA) recognized that there were many unmet mental health needs of our returning soldiers (Baker & Pickren, 2007; Ciarrochi & Bailey, 2008). However, as Baker and Pickren pointed out, there was a shortage of psychiatrists to provide these services. Subsequently, the VA in conjunction with the National Institute of Mental Health (NIMH) began to increase funding for the mental health services and turned to psychologists to assist in this endeavor. Still, at this time psychiatrists and psychologists were enamored with Freudian psychoanalysis (Ciarrochi & Bailey, 2008).

One of Freud's cases in particular that served as a bridge to our current topic of REBT/CBT is that of Little Hans. Hans was 5 years old at the time. Hans' father contacted Freud about his son's phobia of horses. He had once heard someone say not to touch a horse or it will bite off your finger. When walking with his mother, Hans saw a horse fall down and thought it was dead. Freud (1909) wrote about this case demonstrating how Hans was actually jealous of his father. Freud wrote that the horse represented his father. His father's mustache was depicted by the black around the horse's mouth, and his father's glasses were depicted by the horse's blinders. Hans had engaged in masturbation and said he wanted to see his mother's penis. For Freud, this was a classic case demonstrating his belief in the Oedipus complex and how sexual urges were the foundation of phobias.

One of Freud's initial followers, Joseph Wolpe, served in the South African Army during World War II and was charged with treating soldiers with what we now know as Posttraumatic Stress Disorder (PTSD). He came to the realization that he was not having success with the Freudian approach. He subsequently wrote a serious critique of Freud's analysis of Little Hans

(Wolpe & Rachman, 1960) and began his own quest for explaining and treating phobias that was based on Pavlovian and Skinnerian conditioning. He moved to the United States and became a pioneer in behaviorism. This first movement away from Freudian psychoanalysis is considered the *first wave* challenge to psychoanalysis when behaviorism became prominent in understanding the basis of human actions (Ciarrochi & Bailey, 2008; Hayes, 2004a; Plum & Hebblewaite, 2013; Storaasli, Kraushaar, Wilson, & Emrick, 2007). Hayes (2004a) defined a *wave* as "a set or formulation of dominant assumptions, methods, and goals, some implicit, that help organize research, theory, and practice (p. 640).

Criticisms against strict behaviorism began to emerge (Bandura, 1974) and, as mentioned in Chapter 2, it was Ellis and Beck who recognized that cognitive variables also needed to be taken into consideration when examining human emotions and behaviors (Beck, Rush, Shaw, & Emery, 1979; Ellis, 1962, 1971a, 1977a, 2004). Sperry (1993) claimed that the "paradigmatic shift to cognitivism-mentalism, following centuries of rigorous materialism, is bound to have far-reaching consequences" (p. 879). This *cognitive revolution* is the *second wave* of behavior therapy (Ciarrochi & Bailey, 2008; Hayes, 2004a, 2004b; Sperry, 1993; Storaasli et al., 2007).

While still recognizing the importance of cognitions in therapy, more recently, counselors began questioning the need of directly challenging these irrational or negative beliefs (Longmore & Worrell, 2007). This has led to the *third wave* of cognitive behavioral therapy (Bhanji, 2011; Claessens, 2010; Cullen, 2008; Hayes, 2004a; Howells, 2010; Öst, 2008). In these therapies, the focus is not so much on *what* a person thinks, rather on *how* a person thinks. As Ciarrochi and Bailey (2008) mused, therapy has moved from the client lying on a couch with the counselor questioning her or him about childhood experiences to the counselor guiding the client to *mindfully* eat a raisin. In this chapter, I begin by discussing the core concept of mindfulness before going on to discuss important new schools of cognitive and behavioral approaches—Mindfulness-Based Stress Reduction, Mindfulness-Based Cognitive Therapy, Dialectical Behavioral Therapy, and Acceptance and Commitment Therapy. I conclude with research on the latest in neuroscientific findings as they relate to cognitive and behavioral approaches.

Mindfulness

As discussed in Chapter 2, in his early career Albert Ellis was very skeptical about the compatibility of religious beliefs and a healthy emotional life (Ellis, 1976, 2010). However, he later acknowledged that he was open to spiritual philosophies, provided they were not rooted in a one-sided dogmatism or fanaticism (Nielsen, Johnson, & Ellis, 2001). In fact, Christopher (2003) argued that Ellis and Buddha might be considered *soul mates* because of the compatibility between the tenets of REBT and the practices of Zen Buddhism. In particular is Buddhist mindfulness meditation. For this reason, a brief overview of Buddhism gives you insights into the connection with Third Wave CBT.

While Buddhism is a "plural tradition" (Dreyfus, 2011, p. 42), its origin can be traced back to the 5th century BCE when Siddhartha Guatama, a wealthy Indian coming from the privileged class, began his quest to understand suffering in the world (Bodhi, 1998). His teaching became known as *Dhamma* (*Dharma*). At the heart of the teachings are Four Noble Truths (Bodhi, 1998; Teasdale & Chaskalson, 2011a, 2011b). Bodhi (1998, 2011a, 2011b) described these Truths. The First of these is recognizing that mental and physical suffering does exist (*dukkha*). The Second deals with the origin of suffering. Suffering comes from ignorance, greed, and craving (*tanha*). The Third deals with eliminating ignorance through gaining wisdom (*nibbāna, nirvāna*). Finally, wisdom is gained by following the Noble Eightfold path (see Table 3.1):

Table 3.1   Noble Eightfold Path of Striving

1. Right View
2. Right Intention
3. Right Speech
4. Right Action
5. Right Livelihood
6. Right Effort
7. Right Mindfulness
8. Right Concentration

According to Bodhi (1998), mindfulness has a depth of meaning; it is more a "lucid awareness" (p. 19). He translated one of Buddha's specific teachings about mindfulness:

> And what, monks is right mindfulness? Here, a monk dwells on contemplating the body in the body, ardent, clearly comprehending, mindful, having removed covetousness and displeasure in regard to the world. He dwells contemplating feelings in feelings . . . contemplating mind in mind . . . contemplating phenomena in phenomena, ardent, clearly comprehending, mindful, having removed covetousness and displeasure in regard to the world. This is called right mindfulness. (p. 20)

Mindfulness-Based Stress Reduction

As a student of Zen master Seung Sahn, Jon Kabat-Zinn (2011) recognized the healing power of mindfulness meditation. He was most interested in introducing *dharma* into the clinical setting, and in 1979 he founded the Stress Reduction Clinic at the University of Massachusetts Medical School (Kabat-Zinn, 2003, 2005, 2009, 2011). Here in this medical school, Mindfulness-Based Stress Reduction (MBSR) emerged.

Participants who come for this training engage in an intensive 8-week program (Baer, 2003; Fjorback, Arendt, Ørnbøl, Fink, & Walach, 2011; Kabat-Zinn, 1982). They are invited to cultivate mindfulness though formal practices such as sitting meditations, mindful yoga, and lying body scans. In the body scan, they are instructed to focus on all aspects of their body from the toes through the entire body. There are weekly 2- to 2.5-hour sessions and a whole-day retreat. They are asked to practice mindfulness meditations each day for 45 to 60 minutes. However, even during everyday activities such as walking, standing, and eating, participants are encouraged to practice mindfulness.

Kabat-Zinn (2003) defined *mindfulness* as "the awareness that emerges through paying attention on purpose, in the present moment, and nonjudgmentally to the unfolding of experience moment by moment" (p. 145). It does however have a cognitive component involving comprehension and discernment (Dreyfus, 2011; Williams & Kabat-Zinn, 2011). The awareness focuses on what one may see, touch and/or feel, hear, taste, smell, or think (Olendzki, 2011). It begins with conscious breathing (Hanh, 1992; Kabat-Zinn, 2009).

Try it for yourself. Slowly breathe in and out. Be aware of your breathing. Concentrate on breathing in and out. Be aware of your breathing in. Think to yourself, "I am breathing in." Be aware of your breathing out. Think to yourself, "I am breathing out." If you are distracted by your mind wandering or ruminating, try to refocus on your breath without self-criticism and with kindness. Hanh (1992) suggests reciting these four lines as you breathe in and out. "Breathing in, I calm my body. Breathing out, I smile. Dwelling in the present moment, I know this is a wonderful moment!" (p. 10).

Clinical Evidence.   This renewed interest in the mind-body connection, blending meditative practices with medical science, is a convergence of two ways of viewing the world. The appearance of scientific studies examining the effects of MBSR has grown exponentially over the past 30+ years (Kabat-Zinn, 2003, 2009). Initially, MBSR studies examined the effects on chronic pain. Kabat-Zinn (1982) began with 51 patients who were suffering from chronic pain such as facial, shoulder, neck, back, headache, and angina. Various measures of pain indices as well as nonpain psychiatric and mood disturbances were completed by the patients after completing the MBSR course as well as follow-ups at 2.5, 7, and 11 months. Results indicated that the majority of patients reported significant reduction of pain, which continued at follow-up. MBSR can reduce pain symptoms.

In a similar study, Kabat-Zinn, Lipworth, and Burney (1985) compared results of chronic pain patients who were trained in MBSR with patients who being treated by other methods such as physical therapy, Transcutaneous Electrical Nerve Stimulation (TENS), and medications. Again, many measures of pain indices, anxiety, depression, drug utilization, and self-esteem were given pre- and posttreatment and follow-ups. Once more, the MBSR group showed significant improvement compared to the control group and these improvements continued at follow-up.

MBSR was also found to be successful in reducing the time of healing skin lesions for patients with psoriasis who were receiving ultra-violet light treatment (Kabat-Zinn et al., 1998), for reducing distress in and improving mental health in nonclinical samples (Evans, Ferrando, Carr, & Haglin, 2011; Greeson et al., 2011), reducing rumination in cancer patients (Campbell, Labelle, Bacon, Faris, & Carlson, 2012), and increasing self-compassion in a non-clinical population (Birnie, Speca, & Carlson, 2010).

Grossman, Niemann, Schmidt, and Walach (2004) conducted a meta-analysis of 20 MBSR studies involving patients with a wide range of clinical problems such as depression, anxiety, fibromyalgia, binge eating, and chronic pain. They concluded that MBSR is an efficacious treatment for many patients who have both clinical and nonclinical diagnosis.

Another meta-analytic study was done by Ledesma and Kumano (2009). They examined 10 studies that investigated the effectiveness of MBSR on the physical and mental health of patients diagnosed specifically with cancer. Of these, four were randomized controlled trials and six were not. Their results suggested that MBSR is very helpful for improving the mental health of cancer patients, although they concluded that more research may be warranted to show evidence in improving the physical health of cancer patients.

More recently, Fjorback et al. (2011) conducted a meta-analysis of 17 studies with randomized control trials involving MBSR. These authors concluded that MBSR for nonclinical patients was effective in improving mental health in all four of the studies. For clients with physical illnesses including multiple sclerosis, various cancers, chronic obstructive lung disease (COPD), rheumatoid arthritis, fibromyalgia, and HIV, positive results were shown in 9 of the 11 studies. In three of the studies, MBSR was equally effective as the control groups. The exceptions were with patients with COPD and rheumatoid arthritis.

Subsequent to these meta-analytic reviews, there have been many studies that continued to demonstrate the efficacy of MSBR. In the study of Henderson et al. (2012), women with early stage breast cancer were randomized into either MSBR, a nutritional education program (NEP), or usual supportive care (UC). Numerous measures including quality of life (QOL), coping skills, anxiety, personal growth or spirituality depression, and emotional acceptance were taken prior to treatment, after the treatment, and at follow-ups at 12 and 24 months. The MBSR groups showed significant improvement in QOL and coping measures compared to both the NEP and UC groups suggesting the benefits of MBSR. Likewise, Matchim, Armer, and Stewart (2011) found that cancer patients who participated in MBSR had lower cortisol levels and reported less stress. Similarly, Garland, Tamagawa, Todd, Speca, and Carlson (2013) found that MBSR decreased levels of stress in patients diagnosed with cancer. In comparing MBSR with CBT, Arch et al. (2013) found that although both treatments were significantly effective in reducing symptoms of anxiety, CBT may be more helpful in high anxiety patients, whereas MBSR was slightly more effective in patients with high levels of worry or other mood disorders.

In nonclinical populations, persons who participated in MBSR showed an increase in self-compassion, improved emotional regulation, were less absent-minded (Baer, Carmody, & Hunsinger, 2012), and reported lower levels of stress (Robbins, Keng, Ekblad, & Brantley, 2011).

Mindfulness-Based Cognitive Therapy

After corresponding with John Kabat-Zinn about his work, Zindel Segal, Mark Williams and John Teasdale visited him in 1993 and they were invited to observe how MBSR classes were taught (Kabat-Zinn, 2005; Segal, Williams, & Teasdale, 2002). The three had been trained in CBT and knew that it had been shown to be an effective treatment for persons who are diagnosed with depression by challenging irrational beliefs or charting negative thoughts. However, they were interested in exploring the possibility of introducing mindfulness with their clients who had previously been treated for depression as a means of preventing relapse (Kabat-Zinn, 2005; Segal et al., 2002). They believed that persons, even when not experiencing full depression, could be taught to investigate their emotional experiences such as sadness and anger without the need to fix them, thereby avoiding the downward spiral into another full depressive episode. For this purpose, they developed a manualized group skills training program for what is now known as *mindfulness-based cognitive therapy* (MBCT; Segal et al., 2002).

Participants receiving MBCT meet weekly in a group for two-hour sessions that are modeled on MBSR for a period of eight weeks. Without explanation of the goal of the experience, the first session begins with each person in the group receiving a raisin. The group is led through the exercise of slowly examining it, feeling it, smelling it, putting it into their mouth, and finally eating it. The members are then asked to describe their experiences and thoughts. This is followed by a body scan exercise and discussion. The members are given a body scan tape to practice at home. Homework is a very important part of each session. The final exercise is a breath-focused exercise. Each subsequent session builds, and various exercises are introduced that include walking meditations, seeing and hearing meditations, poetry reading, filling out automatic thoughts questionnaires, and viewing and discussing the video *Healing From Within* (Segal et al., 2002).

Clinical Evidence. In their initial research evaluating the effectiveness of MBCT, Teasdale et al. (2000) randomly assigned 145 persons who had recently recovered from depression to either treatment as usual (TAU) or treatment that added MBCT training. Compared to the TUA group, relapse was significantly reduced for those in the MBCT group who had three or more episodes of depression. For those with only two episodes, there was no significant difference.

Ma and Teasdale (2004) attempted to replicate the Teasdale et al. (2000) study as well as to explore why MBCT was not more effective with those persons who had only two episodes of depression. Persons were randomly assigned to either the MBCT or TAU group. Again, the relapse rate for those with three or more episodes of depression was significantly better for the MBCT group (36%) than the TAU group (78%). Their analysis of those with only two episodes of depression suggested that they were not similar to those with three or more episodes regarding time of onset and that the depression was related more specifically to some major life event.

Segal et al. (2010) also found that MBSR was as effective with patients who had been in remission from depression and not receiving antidepressant medication as patients who were being treated with antidepressant medication. In addition to MBCT being equally effective as antidepressant medication, Kuyken et al. (2008) found that the quality of life in the MBCT group had improved.

Since the above studies were conducted by the persons who had developed the treatment, others (Bondolfi et al., 2010; Godfrin & van Heeringen, 2010) wanted to see if the results could be replicated by persons who had not been involved MBCT's development. Both Bondolfi et al. (2010) and Godfrin and van Heeringen (2010) also found that relapse time was significantly delayed in the MBCT group compared to the TAU group.

Therapeutic Alliance.   As mentioned in Chapter 1, Bordin's (1979) notion of bonds, goals, and tasks as the necessary components of the therapeutic relationship was shown to be found in traditional REBT/CBT. The same is true for MBCT.

Felder, Dimidjian and Segal (2012) discussed how collaboration is central to MBCT. Prior to the first group session, the counselor explains the rationale for MBCT and reminds the individual that although the counselor at times may be teaching, it is the individual participant who is the real expert in living with his or her mood disorder.

Felder et al. (2012) explain that "mindfulness practices are led with a spirit of collaboration and mutuality" (p. 180). This collaboration is evidenced in the *inquiry* component of MBCT. This inquiry process is seen when the group counselor engages each in a dyadic conversation regarding his or her "moment-to-moment experiences of each mindfulness practice" (p. 179). Participants are asked to examine whatever thoughts, sensations, or emotions that may have occurred during the practice they have just experienced. The counselor also asks how the practice was different from their typical manner of behaving and how the practice might help in preventing relapse into depression. Even when the counselor asks about struggles a person may have with one of the practices, the group members also provide support by discussing their own difficulties. Collaboration and mutuality are also evident when the counselor not only guides each practice, but also participates.

Dialectical Behavioral Therapy

In the 1970s, Dialectical Behavioral Therapy (DBT) was developed by Marsha Linehan as a form of CBT that was focused on treating patients diagnosed with borderline personality disorder (BPD) who were chronically suicidal (Linehan, 1987, 1993a, 1993b; Lynch & Cuper, 2010). Her contention was that persons with suicidal ideation lacked the necessary skills to build a meaningful life. In addition, she believed that these patients experienced stressors both personal and within the environment. In DBT, the role of the therapeutic relationship becomes a "potent environmental factor" based on radical acceptance of the client but one that focuses on helping that person achieve a goal of changing. Thus, the term dialectic: I accept you, but I want to encourage you to change.

As a treatment for persons diagnosed with BPD, DBT was designed as a manualized program that encompasses various modes of interaction. It involves a commitment to treatment goals on the part of both the counselor and client. In individual therapy, the counselor uses traditional CBT and exposure techniques. However, Linehan (1993a) suggested that acceptance of the patient is most essential. Linehan (1993a) recommended that the counselor use specific dialectical strategies that are aimed at enhancing the therapeutic alliance. In a recent conference, Linehan (2012) reiterated that the only goal a DBT counselor insists on is that the client stay alive until the next session. She explained that she did not initially intend to develop a specific treatment but to show that cognitive and behavioral treatments would be effective. The manual was actually written by observing the sessions and writing down what worked.

Dialectical (Irreverent Communication) Strategies

Linehan (1993a) encourages counselors to engage patients in *paradoxical* dialogue regarding their thoughts and behaviors. For example, "the counselor may say, 'If I didn't care for you, I would try to save you.' The patient may say, 'How can you say that you care for me if you won't save me when I am so desperate?'" (p. 207). In actuality, the patient must realize that the counselor cannot, in fact, save the patient.

Likewise, Linehan (1993a) explained that using *metaphors* is very helpful in DBT. For example, in describing how certain behaviors can interfere with progress, the counselor may talk about a "mountain climber's refusing to wear winter gear when climbing in the snow" (p. 210).

Similar to Ellis's disputation of irrational beliefs, Linehan (1993a) describes this in DBT as playing the *devil's advocate* role. The counselor may argue that the client doesn't really want to change since it is a painful process then asks the client for reasons that the counselor may be wrong.

Another dialectical strategy that is used in DBT is *extending* (Linehan, 1993a). Using this strategy, the counselor relates to the patient that he or she is taken very seriously, perhaps even more seriously than the patient takes herself or himself. This results in the counselor commenting that the patient may even want to fire her or him.

Linehan (1993a, 1993b) explained that it is important for persons with BPD to believe they have the capacity to develop a *wise mind*. This is the ability to make choices and decisions that are not based simply on emotions or reason. Rather a balance between the two. It might be described as an "aha" moment that comes after some crisis. It "may be experienced as grasping the whole picture instead of only the parts" (Linehan, 1993a, p. 215).

Another dialectical strategy that Linehan (1993a) suggested is "*making lemonade out of lemons*" (p. 216). A client's weakness may be seen as a strength. Stubbornness may be turned into action for good. However, it should not be used to humiliate the client.

Problem-Solving Strategies

At the heart of DBT are strategies that are aimed at helping persons generate possible alternative coping skills (Linehan, 1993a, 1993b). In group, this first involves helping the participants do a *behavioral analysis* of the problem situation. What caused the problem? What stands in the way of a solution? Once the problem has been identified, a *chain analysis* is done to determine the specific events that led up to the situation.

For example, consider that Denise becomes extremely irate at her father-in-law. The precipitating event was his recent visit. He had a look of disgust when he came in from the yard and looked around the living room. Denise had the thought that the lawn needed to be mowed, the toys were all around the room, and the room needed painting. She became sad and ashamed and thought to herself that she must really be a loser. She then yelled at her father-in-law and told him he should come around more often and help out. He didn't agree, and then Denise lost her cool and screamed back.

In the case of Denise, the external event of her father-in-law's visit led to a series of painful thoughts and emotions. She will need to recognize each of these to better regulate her emotions.

Validation Strategies

Validation is a way of letting clients know that their responses are understandable or reasonable given their history or situation (Linehan, 1993a, 1993b). Validation strategies require that the counselor strives to find some grain of truth in the client's response even if the behavior seems to be self-defeating. It involves being unbiased, empathetic, and accepting of the client. A client who had a history of being physically abused as a child and reported for hitting his child may be validated by the counselor telling him that while the behavior might not be acceptable, it is understandable given what he learned as a child.

Commitment Strategies

Linehan (1987, 1993a) described a number of ways that the counselor should continually try to motivate the client to change. In addition to having the client evaluate the pros and cons of changing, while allowing the client the freedom to commit or not, she suggests that with the *foot-in-the-door* technique, client agreement on a small goal may eventually lead to agreement on a larger one. Similarly, when the client does not agree to a rather large goal, the *door-in-the-face* technique increases the probability that the client will agree to a smaller one. The counselor also acts as the devil's advocate, encouraging the client to accept the challenge of changing.

In addition to individual therapy, those in the DBT treatment program participate in group skills training modules. There are specific acceptance skills and change skills that are taught in sequence with specific handouts and homework assignments.

Mindfulness Skills Module

Linehan was also trained in the practice of Zen (Lynch & Cuper, 2010) and considers mindfulness skills as core to DBT (Linehan, 1993a, 1993b). These core mindfulness skills are described as *whats* and *hows*.

Persons are first taught to observe or attend to their behaviors, emotions, and external events without trying to change them. In group, they are then instructed to describe in words their emotions, behaviors, and responses to events. As in traditional REBT/CBT, they are taught that emotions are not the direct result of the external events but rather the cognitions. Finally, they discuss what it means to participate in an activity without being self-conscious about it. Think about something like riding a bike. Once you have this skill, you can get on your bike without being conscious about how to balance yourself.

Once the persons in the group are exposed to the *what* skills, they are reminded that *how* they attend, describe, and participate is very important. They are led to understand the importance of being nonjudgmental, that is, without evaluating behaviors and emotions as being either good or bad. They are then exposed to practicing how to focus on one specific task at a time rather than being distracted by other thoughts or worries. Finally, they are presented with the goal of being effective, doing what works rather than having to be right. It involves learning how to "read" people. It is explained as being the opposite of "cutting off your nose to spite your face" (Linehan, 1993b, p. 65).

Interpersonal Effectiveness Skills Module

In this next 8-week module, persons are presented with ways of being more socially effective (Linehan, 1993a, 1993b, 1995). Throughout this module they are presented with an acronym to help remind them of things they need to practice (see Table 3.2).

Table 3.2   DEARMAN

D	**Describe** your current situation that you may be reacting to
E	**Express** your feelings and opinions: "I feel that I have worked hard enough to get a raise"
A	**Assert** yourself by asking or saying "No"
R	**Reinforce** and **reward** persons ahead of time: "I will really appreciate your understanding"
M	Be **Mindful** of objectives without distraction
A	**Appear** effective and competent
N	**Negotiate** alternatives

Emotional Regulation Skills Module

In this next module, persons are led to understand that it is possible for them to both tolerate and regulate even intense emotional reactions by recognizing the function of such emotions. They are taught to identify and label their emotions and recognize any obstacles that might stand in the way of changing. They practice being mindful of their current emotions and are encouraged to act in ways that might seem contrary to the emotions, such as being kind to a person who seems to be making them angry. Like in the Interpersonal Effectiveness module, persons are reminded of an acronym to help reduce their vulnerability (Linehan, 1993a, 1993b, 1995).

Table 3.3   PLEASE

P and L	Treat any **PhysicaL** illness
E	**Eat** a balanced diet
A	**Avoid** mood-altering drugs (unless medical condition warrants)
S	Set a regular **Sleep** pattern
E	**Exercise** regularly

Distress Tolerance Skills Module

The final module is aimed at helping persons be able to tolerate the discomfort that they may experience without demanding that things change. They are presented with strategies to help them survive a distressful crisis, but they are not used for emotional regulation. The first group of strategies is aimed at distracting the person from the stressful event. Again, an acronym: ACCEPTS (Linehan, 1993a, 1993b, 1995).

Table 3.4   ACCEPTS

A	**Activities** can be distracting in a healthy way	Go for a walk, garden, fish, play golf
C	**Contribute** and **Commit** to positive actions based on your personal values	Volunteer at a soup kitchen or homeless shelter
C	**Compare** yourself with someone who may be less well off than you are	Think of persons from a recent tornado
E	Find activities that may help you experience an opposite **Emotion**	Go to an emotional movie, read emotional books, listen to emotional music
P	**Push** yourself away from the situation by leaving it or blocking it in your mind	Try putting your pain in a locked box
T	Distract by trying to change your **Thoughts**	Count the tiles on the floor, count to 20 backwards
S	Make other **Sensations** more intense	Put an ice cube on your neck, swim in cold water, take a hot shower

Another set of strategies in this module involves self-soothing. The focus here is to help the person attend to the five senses of seeing, hearing, smelling, tasting, and touching.

Finally, this module helps persons find ways to improve their present moment. These include cognitive techniques that help persons reframe or change their evaluation or appraisal of the situation. The acronym is IMPROVE (Linehan, 1993a, 1995).

Table 3.5   IMPROVE

I	**Imagery** can help create a safe and secure environment
M	Discovering **Meaning** in one's life is often helpful even if a person is not religious
P	**Prayer** may be a way of expressing radical acceptance of oneself by asking "Why me?"
R	**Relaxation** techniques/tapes may prove to be helpful
O	Remember to take **One** thing at a moment
V	Take a **Vacation** from adulthood for a moment
E	**Encourage** yourself

Clinical Evidence

In the initial research examining the effectiveness of DBT, Linehan, Armstrong, Suarez, Allmon, and Heard (1991) studied 47 women who were chronically suicidal and diagnosed with BPD and were randomly assigned to either DBT or TAU. While persons in both groups showed fewer symptoms of depression, hopelessness, and suicidal ideation, as well as improvement in reasons for living, the persons in the DBT group had fewer suicidal attempts, were more likely to remain in treatment, and had fewer inpatient hospitalization stays.

A second randomly controlled trial (RCT) was conducted involving women who were diagnosed with BPD who were also drug-dependent (Linehan et al., 1999). Again, they either received DBT or TAU. As in the above study, women in the DBT group were more likely to remain in treatment. Results also indicated that the drug use was significantly reduced for the women in the DBT group. They also showed greater gains on measures of social adjustment.

Another RCT was conducted by Linehan et al. (2002). These authors compared the effectiveness of DBT with a Comprehensive Validation Therapy, which included a 12-Step component with a group of women who were diagnosed with BPD and were also addicted to heroin. Unlike the above studies, the women in the DBT group were less likely to remain in treatment. However, while both treatment groups were effective in reducing opiate use, those in the DBT group maintained the reduction at the end of the 12-month period.

DBT was also compared to community treatment by persons who were experts in working with persons who were suicidal (Linehan et al., 2006). Women were randomly assigned to either DBT or enhanced cognitive-behavioral therapy (CBTE). Persons in both groups reported fewer symptoms of depressions. However, the women in the DBT group were more likely to remain in treatment and were less likely to be hospitalized for suicidal ideation.

In addition to the studies by Linehan and her colleagues, there are a number of other researchers who have replicated findings that demonstrated the effectiveness of DBT (Axelrod, Perepletchikova, Holtzman, & Sinha, 2011; Koons et al., 2001).

Therapeutic Alliance

To Linehan (1993a, 1993b), the therapeutic relationship is absolutely essential. She and her colleagues recognized that it is a *common factor* that needed to be examined as a mechanism of change (Bedics, Atkins, Comtois, & Linehan, 2012). In addition, the relationship "*is* also the therapy" (Linehan, 1993a, p. 514). For the relationship to develop, the DBT counselor will need to be "sensitive, flexible, non-judgmental, accepting, and patient" (Linehan, 1993a, p. 514). She went to length to provide strategies for developing this relationship (1993a). It begins with accepting the client in the current moment and being willing to enter into the client's struggles and pain. When the relationship becomes problematic for either the client or counselor, it is to be approached as a problem to be solved. Linehan (1993a) suggested that generalizations from the relationship be applied to the client's everyday life.

Not only does the relationship develop within the individual and group sessions, but also within the natural environment of the client (Lynch, Chapman, Rosenthal, Kuo, & Linehan, 2006). These authors explained that part of the DBT treatment includes contacting the counselor by telephone as a way of reinforcing the skills and reducing suicidal ideation. In addition, they are meant to provide the client with the opportunity to deal with any disruption in the therapeutic relationship.

In conclusion, counselors following the DBT model focus on acceptance and change, treat the whole client (not disease or disorder), and reinforce adaptive behaviors in a nurturing environment. It is important that both the counselor and client believe the client is empowered.

Acceptance and Commitment Therapy

In contrast to the traditional CBT approaches that encourage clients to challenge and change their thoughts and feelings, Acceptance and Commitment Therapy, or ACT, as initially developed by Steven Hayes, focuses on helping clients simply notice and accept these experiences (Hayes, 2004a, 2004b; Hayes, Strosahl, & Wilson, 2012; Springer, 2012; Waltz & Hayes, 2010). An ACT counselor views attempts to change one's thoughts *as the problem* rather than the solution. In turn, the ACT counselor will help clients choose a valued direction and act on making that value come to fruition (Hayes, 2004a, 2004b). Like the other third wave therapies described in this chapter, ACT utilizes mindfulness strategies to help clients become aware of their cognitions and sensations. In addition, ACT emphasizes acceptance and behavioral strategies with the goal of improving *psychological flexibility*. Hayes et al. (2012) defined this as "contacting the present moment as a conscious human being, fully and without needless defense—as it is and not what it says it is—and persisting with or changing behaviors in the service of chosen values" (pp. 96–97). This may be understood as the ability a person has to become engaged in behaviors that are value-based even while being fully and consciously in touch with the present thoughts, emotions, or sensations.

ACT is an outgrowth of relational frame theory (RFT), which posits that human beings learn by relating things or events to each other (Hayes,

2004a, 2004b; Hayes et al., 2012). Initially, a child may say that a dime is less than a nickel but when the child goes to buy something that costs 10 cents, the child realizes that the context of function makes a difference. Language functions are seen to dominate especially when rules come into play and this may lead to an inflexibility. How can one alter these language processes that lead to inflexibility?

As a way of promoting *psychological flexibility*, ACT targets six core complementary interrelated processes:

1. *Acceptance* is contrasted with *experiential avoidance*. It is the willingness to be aware, in a nonjudgmental way, of any of your inner states such as thoughts, feelings, and bodily sensations. However, it is not to be misunderstood as tolerance of injustices.

2. *Defusion* is contrasted with *cognitive fusion*. Hayes (2010) offered a rather explicit example. How much saliva do you think you swallow in a day? What if you filled a half-cup with your saliva? What is your reaction if you thought you would have to drink it? There is an implicit rule that saliva is not for human consumption. This is cognitive fusion. On the other hand, consider a man who has been diagnosed with a malignant brain tumor. Suppose he thinks to himself that his life is now worthless. If these words lead him to avoid his favorite sport of golf, that would be fusion, but if he undermined the power of those words and went out with his buddies to play golf that would be defusion. Defusion takes place when psychological processes can make a difference in the way one behaves.

3. *Self as context* is contrasted with the conceptualized self. Can you experience the continuity of yourself from last year? The time you were a teenager? How about your earliest memories as a child?

4. *Contact with the present moment* is contrasted with rigid attention to past or future events. It is the ability to be aware in a nonjudgmental way of the actual here and now. Try being focused on the room you are sitting in. What sounds do you hear?

5. *Clarifying values* that are freely chosen is contrasted with behaviors that are rule-governed. What would you like to have written on your tombstone?

6. *Committed action* is choosing to take an action "*with* reason" as compared to "*for* reasons" (Waltz & Hayes, 2010, pp. 164–165). It is commitment to act in a way that is an outgrowth of the client's values. If you value personal self-care, how often do you go to the gym or take time for yourself?

Clinical Evidence

By 2004, preliminary data began to emerge showing that ACT was an effective treatment for a number of different conditions (Hayes, Masuda, Bissett, Luoma, Guerrero, 2004). This included reducing the number of hair pullings for persons with trichotillomania (Twohig & Woods, 2004), reduction of sick-leave and medical visits for persons with stress and pain symptoms (Dahl, Wilson, & Nilsson, 2004), increasing tolerance for persons with chronic pain (Gutiérrez, Luciano, Rodríguez, & Fink, 2004), and for increasing levels of smoking cessation (Gifford et al., 2004).

The clinical evidence in support of ACT has continued to mount (Arch et al., 2013; Forman, Herbert, Moitra, Yeomans, & Geller, 2007; Petersen & Zettle, 2009; Twohig et al., 2010). But how does it compare with traditional CBT? In a meta-analytic review, Ruiz (2012) looked at 16 studies that compared the gold standard traditional CBT with ACT on a variety of measures. Although there were many limitations to this study, results suggested that while there were no significant differences on measures of anxiety, there was a positive trend for ACT on measures of depression.

Therapeutic Alliance

The therapeutic alliance (TA) is central to ACT. It is a collaborative effort based on trust (Lejuez, Hopko, Levine, Gholkar, & Collins, 2006). Although not an end in itself, it is considered a vehicle of change. It demands radical respect and honors diversity (Hayes et al., 2012).

Because the ACT counselor is not intent on changing the client's cognitions, Hayes (2004b) challenges the ACT counselor to "do as you say (rather) than say what you do" (p. 651) when feelings of frustration or confusion arise in therapy. In other words, the counselor learns to walk in the shoes of her client. Hayes concluded that "because of this quality, the therapeutic relationship is important, powerful, and deliberately equal in ACT" (p. 652). This relationship will require that both the counselor and the client develop cognitive flexibility (Hayes et al., 2012).

There is a two-mountain metaphor that has been used to describe the trusting and collaborative therapeutic alliance in ACT:

> The counselor and the patient are conceptualized as climbing their own separate mountains. While the counselor can help the patient, it is stressed that the counselor is an individual who has problems climbing his or her own mountain. Thus, while the counselor may be vulnerable to traps and pitfalls on his or her own mountain, the counselor does have a unique view of the patient's mountain that may be useful for assisting the patient in their struggles. Thus, as with TA, ACT is not hierarchical but instead a collaborative process. (Lejuez et al., 2006, p. 460)

As in DBT, the therapeutic relationship is at the core of ACT. If you think that you may be interested in becoming an ACT practitioner, you will be opening yourself to relationships that are often intense but meaningful. You will be helping your clients recognize that in and beneath their pain lie their deepest values; significantly, from these values often comes their deepest pain. As an ACT practitioner, you will need to reflect on this in your own life as well.

Neuroscience and REBT/CBT

Prior to the 1980s, the brain was considered to be a more permanent and fixed structure. Specific brain regions controlled specific functions. One of the exciting developments in psychotherapy today is research that is integrating the basic assumptions of CBT with the actual neurobiological evidence of brain neuroplasticity (Jokić-Begić, 2010). As Jokić-Begić remarked, the adage that "neurons that fire together, wire together; neurons that fire apart, wire apart" (p. 238) has gained much attention in neuroscience studies, particularly in the case of CBT. Jokić-Begić pointed out that changes in blood flow activity led to the discovery that the brain can actually change and create new neurons and there is a growing body of evidence that the brain may actually change as a result of cognitive behavioral interventions.

This was demonstrated by Paquette et al. (2003), who investigated CBT treatment effects on the fMRI imaging of persons with spider phobia. Prior to treatment, there was abnormal activity in the right dorsolateral area of the prefrontal cortex as well as in the parahippocampal gyrus. These abnormalities disappeared after CBT treatment and normal cortical processing was observed.

Bar (2009) theorized that there is a relationship between mood regulation and cortical activation. He based this on his findings on neuroimaging that revealed changes in three cortical regions: (a) the parahippocampal cortex in the medial temporal lobe, (b) the medial cortex in the parietal lobe, and (c) the medial prefrontal cortex. He proposed that researchers continue to explore this neuroscience hypothesis between mood disorders and depression.

In a longitudinal study, Kumari et al. (2011) examined the functional brain changes in 54 patients diagnosed with schizophrenia and two with schizoaffective disorder. Of these patients, 28 received specific manualized CBT treatment for psychosis, while the remaining 26 received treatment as usual without CBT. At baseline there was no significant difference in functional magnetic resonance imaging (fMRI) of brain activation in both groups. However, for those who received the CBT treatment, fMRI from baseline to follow-up showed a "significant decreased activation of the inferior frontal, insula, thalamus, putamen, and occipital areas" (Kumari et al., 2011, p. 2396).

Newer neurobiological research also suggests that results from fMRI can be predictive of recovery with patients who are diagnosed with depression and are treated with CBT. Functional magnetic resonance imaging results have shown specific healthy changes in brain activity when treating obsessive compulsive disorder, panic disorder, unipolar depression, and spider phobia with CBT (Beauregard, 2009; Zurowski et al., 2012). CBT has been shown to change specific brain regions in the frontal cortex, cingulate, and hippocampus (Goldapple et al., 2004; Siegle, Carter, & Thase, 2006). Likewise, there is evidence that CBT may be considered a feasible alternative with patients who are diagnosed with schizophrenia but not prescribed with antipsychotic medication (Christodoulides, Dudley, Brown, Turkington, & Beck, 2008).

Beck (2008) himself is encouraged by the possibilities for research demonstrating the interaction between genetic, neurochemical, and cognitive factors in the development of depression. He proposed that there are both genetic and neurobiological correlates involved in understanding depression. He focused on research showing that the 5-HTTLPR gene, which is a serotonin transporter, seems to moderate depression. He proposed a hypothetical pathway that begins with the amygdala. He speculated that an amygdala, which is hyperactive combined with hypoactive prefrontal regions of the brain, may be linked to the diminishment of cognitive appraisal, which is associated with the onset of depression. He believes that it is essential to continue examining the evidence of neuroscience. In his own words, "I have reason to hope that future research will perhaps provide a new paradigm which for the first time can integrate findings from psychological and biological studies to build a new understanding of depression" (Beck, 2008, p. 976).

But whatever the evolution of a cognitive model may have regarding the interactions between biological mechanisms and cognitive processing, it is important to look at these developments from the lens of the common factors. Fuchs (2004) reminds us that neuroscience alone does not completely explain the "complex interpersonal process" (p. 484) that occurs during counseling. Even neuroscientists have acknowledged this. Montes (2013) has suggested that future counselors must take into consideration these neuroscientific developments. Yet at the same time he reminds us of what Ryan Melton, clinical training director of Portland State's Research Institute and strong advocate for weaving neuroscientific principles into therapeutic training, has said in this regard: "We still know that we get our best outcomes when we establish a strong therapeutic alliance with our clients" (Montes, 2013, p. 8).

Summary

- Psychologists began to challenge Freudian psychoanalysis and examined behaviors (behaviorism) to understand the basis of human actions; this is known as the first wave. The cognitive revolution, led by Ellis and Beck, was considered the second wave, which now added recognition of the cognitive components needed when examining human behaviors. The third wave of cognitive therapy has less focus on what the person thinks and more focus on how the person feels. This wave led to the development of practices such as MBCT, DBT, and ACT.
- Mindfulness, awareness from paying attention on purpose, has a cognitive component and includes activities such as conscious breathing, meditation, mindful yoga, and lying body scans. The therapeutic relationship is enhanced when the counselor guides and participates in the mindfulness practice.
- DBT is a manualized program developed for BPD that focuses on accepting clients and encouraging them to change. DBT counselors use CBT and exposure techniques as well as paradoxical dialogue, metaphors, the devil's advocate role, and extending to help clients develop alternative coping skills.
- In DBT, the therapeutic relationship *is* also the therapy.
- ACT encourages clients to notice and accept thoughts and feelings and choose a direction and act on meeting the goal. This form of therapy emphasized acceptance and behavioral strategies.
- Neuroscience and neuroplasticity advances have advanced the efficacy of CBT, and it is vital to take the common factors perspective into consideration. Meaning, even neuroscientists found the best results when a strong therapeutic relationship was established with clients.

4

Multiculturalism

Demographics are changing. When the census was taken in 2010, persons were asked to specify their race. There were four main categories to choose from: (1) One race (white, black, American Indian and Alaskan Native [AIAN], Asian, and Native Hawaiian and Other Pacific Islander [NHPI]); (2) Two or more races; (3) Non-Hispanic white alone; or (4) Hispanic. Projections from that U.S. 2010 Census suggested that by 2030 the rate of Non-Hispanic whites will decline by 2.1% per thousand, while those who claim two or more races will increase by 26.3% per thousand. It is also predicted that by 2042 there will be no clear majority because the white population will fall below 50% (Hixson, Hepler, & Kim, 2011).

However, we are not there yet, since presently in the United States there is still a white majority. This white majority has historically come with many advantages and resources. McIntosh (1995) described this as white-skin privilege. She compared it to being "like an invisible weightless knapsack of special provisions, assurances, maps, guides, codebooks, passports, visas, clothes, compass, emergency gear, and blank checks" (McIntosh, 1995, para. 4). Here are a few of the many examples she offered. I paraphrase them as questions to you, the reader:

- Can you go shopping alone and feel assured that you won't be followed or harassed?
- Can you go into a hairdresser's shop and find someone who can deal with your hair?
- If you are pulled over by the police or audited by the IRS, can you be sure you weren't being profiled because of your race?
- If you are hired by an affirmative action employer, will your coworkers suspect it is because of your race?
- Can you buy bandages that are "flesh" colored that nearly match your skin?

How many of your responses are yes? Are any of your answers no? Why do you think this is so? I encourage each of you as perspective counselors who are reading this chapter to reflect on your own personal beliefs, and perhaps even implicit biases, if you wish to become a culturally competent provider. I also ask you to consider your ethical responsibility to be sensitive to and learn about the challenges of multicultural counseling in a male-dominated, white-privileged society.

Emergence of Multicultural Awareness in Counseling and Psychology

Researchers have suggested that the concept of multiculturalism in counseling and psychology was a direct outgrowth of the civil rights movement (Arredondo, Tovar-Blank, & Parham, 2008; Helms, 1994; Makedon, 1996; Pope-Davis & Coleman, 2007; Thompson & Neville, 1999). At this time, a prevailing notion among many counselors was that all human beings should be treated alike regardless of race. This universal approach is known as *etic* (Sue, 1983). Yet, while perhaps an admirable sentiment, it was not practiced in reality (Sue, 1977; Vontress, 1971) and biases remained. In his preface to Pope-Davis and Coleman's (2007) book on multicultural counseling, D. W. Sue highlighted that prior to the 1980s, ethnic minority groups often did not have access to or opportunities to receive mental health services because of biases in mental health practitioners. Sue (1983) recognized the need for an *emic* approach, which takes into consideration the sociocultural values of specific cultures.

The American Psychological Association (APA) also recognized these biases and inadequacies and in 1980 established the Board of Ethnic Minorities Affairs. As an outcome of this, Sue et al. (1982) suggested that one step in overcoming the deficiencies in mental health services and research would be for the APA to adopt cross-cultural competencies for accreditation criteria. These authors proposed a set of guidelines centering on specific beliefs and attitudes, knowledge, and skills that should be incorporated into graduate programs for counselors, psychologists, and other mental health providers.

Sue, Arrendo, and McDavis (1992) provided a conceptual framework for organizing these competencies of a culturally skilled counselor along three dimensions of becoming aware of one's biases, understanding clients without negative judgments, and actively developing strategies and skills in working with culturally different clients. Building on these, Arredondo et al. (1996) proposed that counselors appreciate the complexity of their clients through the lens of a three-dimensional model of personal identity.

One dimension incorporates more permanent characteristics such a person's age, gender, language, physical ability, race, sexual orientation, and social class. Another dimension is the historical context into which a person is born. And the final dimension is the interaction between the dimensions of permanent characteristics and historical context.

With this framework of a Personal Identity Model, Arredondo et al. (1996) listed over 100 explanatory statements to enumerate specific multicultural competencies for counselors. I include a small sample for you to consider. Competent counselors

- can identify specific cultural groups from which counselors derive their fundamental cultural heritage and the specific beliefs and attitudes held by those cultures that are assimilated into their own attitudes and beliefs (para. 50);
- recognize their stereotypical reactions to people different from themselves (e.g., silently articulating their awareness of a negative stereotypical reaction, "I noticed that I locked my car door when that African-American teenager walked by.") (para. 63);
- culturally skilled counselors value bilingualism and do not view another language as an impediment to counseling ("monolingualism" may be the culprit) (para. 72).

These competencies were formally endorsed by both the APA and the American Counseling Association (ACA) and many of these concepts were incorporated into the *ACA Code of Ethics* (American Counseling Association, 2005; Pack-Brown, Thomas, & Seymour, 2008).

Challenges and Contemporary Concerns

The model proposed by Sue et al. (1982) was considered a landmark contribution to the field of counseling and psychology (Chao, 2013). However, both it and the subsequent elaboration of the model by Arredondo et al. (1996) met with challenges. There have been debates about the scope of multiculturalism (e.g., the benefits versus the drawbacks of broadening multiculturalism to include factors such as gender [Helms, 1994; Helms & Carter, 1997]). There have been debates about the empirical validity of some of the competencies and calls for more empirical data (Weinrach & Thomas, 2002).

There have been debates about whether an emic approach tended to become more of a cookbook process wherein specific techniques are emphasized and that may be based on somewhat stereotypical notions (Speight, Myers, Cox, & Highlen, 1991). There has also been concern with developing a tripartite framework of personal identity development, in which each person is unique, belongs to differing groups, and partakes of human universality.

This echoes the sentiment expressed much earlier by Kluckhohn and Murray's (1948) statement that "every man is in certain respects (a) like all other men, (b) like some other men, (c) like no other man" (p. 35).

Regarding clinical practice, D'Andrea and Daniels (2001) provided a multicultural framework that is RESPECTFUL and inclusive:

Table 4.1   RESPECTFUL

R	Religious values
E	Economic/class issues
S	Sexual identity issues
P	Psychological developmental issues
E	Ethnic/racial identity issues
C	Chronological issues
T	Trauma and threats to well-being
F	Family issues
U	Unique physical issues
L	Language and location of residence issues

Similarly, Hays (1996, pp. 332–334) outlined a model that emphasized nine cultural influences in relation to specific minority groups that counselors should be ADDRESSING:

Table 4.2   ADDRESSING

A	Age/generational
D	Disability
R	Religion
E	Ethnicity/race
S	Social status
S	Sexual orientation
I	Indigenous heritage
N	National origin
G	Gender

Culturally Competent REBT/CBT

Prior to his death, a colleague and I e-mailed Albert Ellis asking what he saw as REBT's multicultural contribution to therapy. Ellis (2004) responded that REBT "always favored multi-cultural procedures, because it thinks that bigotry and prejudice are sources of a great deal of human disseverance. Therefore, it looks for bigotry and prejudices in the functioning of both the therapist and the client and does its best to diminish or eliminate such prejudice" (personal communication, June 29, 2004).

Examining multiculturalism from a common factors perspective, Fischer, Jome, and Atkinson (1998) synthesized many empirical articles and delineated four factors that they believed were essential: the therapeutic relationship, the degree to which both counselor and client share a common worldview, the positive expectation of change on the part of the client, and the specific types of interventions that the counselor may suggest. Not every intervention will be relevant for every client. Much will depend on the strength of the therapeutic relationship, the common worldview, and the expectancy of change, and to strengthen each factor, an in-depth understanding of each culturally diverse client is essential.

Much research remains to be done to foster this understanding, since generally speaking, both ethnic and racial minorities, such as African-American, Latino, Asian, American Indian, and Alaskan Indian, have been underrepresented in therapeutic outcome studies. This same is true for other minority groups, such as lesbian, gay, bisexual, transgendered, and questioning (LGBTQ) persons (Balsam, Martell, & Safren, 2006; Lowe & Mascher, 2001; Pantelone, Iwamasa, & Martell, 2009). However, currently there is a small but growing body of evidence demonstrating the efficacy of using REBT/CBT with culturally diverse populations. A number of examples are provided below.

The Latino Culture and BEBT/CBT

The term *Latino* is commonly used to describe persons, either immigrant to the United States or born in this country, from a variety of countries, including Mexico, Puerto Rico, Cuba, as well as other Central and South American countries (Organista, 2006). Although Organista and Muñoz (1996) recognized that "each Latino is in some ways like no other, and that there are subgroups of Latinos that are quite different from one another" (p. 255), they state that "nevertheless, there are elements of shared history, of language, customs, religion and moral values, and of self-identity attributed by others, which define, however imperfectly, a recognizable subgroup in society that must be properly served" (p. 255). These persons most often speak Spanish and have roots in the earlier Spanish settlers and/or indigenous inhabitants (Organista, 2006).

There are traditional Latino values that need to be considered when an REBT/CBT counselor is working with a person from this culture. One in particular is *personalismo*. This refers to the value that is placed on personal relationships in all human interactions, including those that may be professional or task-oriented (Interian & Diaz-Martinez, 2007; Organista, 2006). Roll, Millen, and Martinez (1980) suggested that REBT/CBT counselors need to keep this in mind and recognize the need to give personalized attention to the client before jumping into the immediate task of focusing on the presenting problem. This may involve engaging in *platica* (small talk) to build *confianza* (trust) (Organista & Muñoz, 1996; Roll et al., 1980).

Another central traditional Latino value is *familismo* (González-Prendes, Hindo, & Pardo, 2011; Organista, 2006). This refers to the collective orientation that places family interests and loyalty above one's own. As an example, Organista (2006) suggested that REBT/CBT counselors refrain from suggestions such as "You need to take care of yourself first" (p. 81); since that is "not as culturally compatible as those that link self-care to family care" (p. 81), the REBT/CBT counselor might consider saying, "You can take better care of your family by taking care of yourself" (p. 81).

Rosselló, Bernal, and Rivera-Medina (2008) compared CBT and interpersonal psychotherapy (IPT) as a treatment for depression with a group of adolescents from Puerto Rico in both individual and group settings. They considered how each of these approaches had elements that might find resonance in the Latino culture. The didactic/classroom format of CBT lessens the stigma that is often attached to therapy for *locos* (crazy people), while the focus of IPT is on present interpersonal conflicts. This underscores such values as *familismo* and *personalismo* in the Latin culture. Although both conditions were successful in reducing depressive symptoms, those in the CBT treatments scored significantly lower in depressive symptoms and significantly higher on measures of self-concept.

Another anecdotal case study was provided by Elligan (1997) to illustrate the effectiveness of CBT when working with multicultural clients. His client was a bicultural (Latino/Palestinian) law school student, who was previously diagnosed with dysthymia. He had not made progress in therapy when his counselor was a white male. Elligan on the other hand, a counselor of color, was able to improve the therapeutic alliance by being sensitive to the issues of acculturation. Using CBT, Elligan was able to help his client develop coping skills to deal with the stressors in his life. Elligan found that cognitive restructuring was necessary to remove dysfunctional thoughts. This client struggled with acculturation to the law school, and his stress and negative verbalizations centered on "fitting in" to this environment. After completion of CBT treatment, this client successfully extinguished the negative verbalizations.

Asian Americans and REBT/CBT

Just as Organista and Muñoz (1996) reminded us that the Latino culture has many subgroups, the same is true of the Asian Americans. Included within this population you may find, among others, Pacific Islanders, Chinese, Japanese, Koreans, Taiwanese, Hawaiians, Vietnamese, and Filipinos (Iwamasa, Hsia, & Hinton, 2006; Miller, Yang, & Chen, 1997). While these groups are diverse, the REBT/CBT counselor is encouraged to consider a number of culture-specific values that should be explored.

The family structure in the traditional Asian culture is one that is hierarchical, patriarchal and authoritarian (Iwamasa et al., 2006). It is often the case that children are expected to bring honor to their family through their achievements, and emotional restraint is often emphasized (Chen & Davenport, 2005). The parents of Asian Americans may not openly express emotions, and the children learn that love is expressed by providing materially for the children. In turn, the children are often expected to help with household chores (Iwamasa et al., 2006). Generally speaking, Asian families are more focused on collectivist values rather than on individual needs, evocatively expressed in the Japanese proverb "The protruding nail will be pounded down" (Iwamasa et al., 2006).

Researchers (Chen, 1995; Chen & Davenport, 2005; Lin, 2001) have suggested that many of the tenets of REBT/CBT are very congruent with Asian cultural norms. In the Chinese culture, cognition and logical thinking are paramount. According to Chen (1995), Chinese people value rationality and logic to solve life's many problems. They also emphasize the importance of a person's perception of an event. This is evident in the old Chinese proverb "Originally there is no disturbance in the world, but people make themselves feel worried" (Chen, 1995, p. 120). The role of teacher in Asian culture is one that is highly respected (Chen, 1995). Authority is respected, and authoritative expertise is valued (Lin, 2001). As noted earlier, REBT/CBT has a very strong educational component, and this role of teacher in the Chinese culture is one that is held in great respect (Chen, 1995). Lin also emphasized that Chinese clients are in favor of a directive approach, which is one of the hallmarks of REBT/CBT. This was substantiated by the research of Exum and Lau (1988).

LGBTQ and REBT/CBT

On September 30, 2012, California passed an historic piece of legislation that banned so-called *conversion therapy* aimed at helping minors "overcome" their homosexuality (SB 1172, 2012). Section 1 of the bill asserts that "being lesbian, gay, or bisexual is not a disease, disorder, illness, deficiency, or shortcoming. The major professional associations of mental health practitioners and researchers in the United States have recognized this fact for nearly 40 years." Yet this bill was not met with universal support by mental health providers. In particular was the National Association for Research and Therapy of Homosexuality (NARTH). This organization has issued guidelines for treating persons who have unwanted same-sexual attractions.

In much of the Western world, through most of the 20th century, homosexuality was considered a mental disorder. It was not until 1973 that the Board of Trustees of the APA voted to eliminate homosexuality as a diagnostic category in the *Diagnostic and Statistical Manual of Mental Disorders* (DSM; Greenberg, 1997). Yet, despite the DSM changes on paper, societal hatred and hostility did not disappear. Recall Matthew Shepard, a gay man and victim of antigay hatred. He was kidnapped and tied to a fence on October 7, 1998, where he died 5 days later. Shepard's death has come to symbolize the degree of homophobia in this country (Lowe & Mascher, 2001). Short of death, LGBTQ adults have suffered many other negative effects of discrimination, including depression, anger, anxiety, and posttraumatic stress disorder (Herek, Gillis, & Cogan, 1999). In 2009, the APA Task Force on Appropriate Responses to Sexual Orientation issued a report that examined sexual orientation change efforts (SOCE). The members of the task force reiterated that the sexual stigma that is directed at persons of nonheterosexual orientation is a major source of *minority* stress. They concluded that the "compelling evidence of decreased same-sex sexual behavior was rare" (p. 2) and, more often than not, SOCE participants reported harmful effects.

It is against this backdrop that Balsam et al. (2006) pointed out the advantages of using REBT/CBT with LGBTQ persons.

- There is sufficient evidence that REBT/CBT has been successful in treating anxiety and depression, which is often a presenting problem with LGBTQ persons.
- REBT/CBT focuses on the external activating events in a person's life and does not pathologize LGBTQ as an intrapsychic disorder.
- REBT/CBT is a collaborative effort between the client and counselor giving the client a voice that she or he may not experience in the heterosexist society.
- REBT/CBT offers skills-training tools to cope with the stress and anxiety.
- REBT/CBT accepts individuals without judgment.
- REBT/CBT can help LGBTQ persons dispute any homophobic beliefs that may have been internalized.

Safren and Rogers (2001) discussed a number of guidelines that REBT/CBT counselors should consider when working with LGBTQ persons. To begin, counselors are encouraged to examine their own attitudes and beliefs about LGBTQ persons. The authors emphasized the importance of assessing the role that sexual orientation plays with the client. It may or may not be a presenting problem. Also, they pointed out the importance in acknowledging how social norms often underlie the negative irrational beliefs that are associated with being attracted to a person of the same sex. Finally, they encouraged counselors to evaluate for the absence or presence of social support networks for the persons.

Safren and Rogers (2001) offered two case studies demonstrating the effectiveness of CBT with LGBTQ persons. The first case was Michael, a gay male presenting with social phobia. He wanted to meet other gay males but avoided situations where it might be possible. Safren had Michael develop a fear hierarchy related to situations that he avoided. Therapy included role-playing about those anxiety-provoking situations as well as actual in vivo exposures. Safren continued to dispute Michael's irrational beliefs throughout therapy treatments by asking questions such as "Where is the evidence that this is actually true?" (Safren & Rogers, 2001, p. 635). After 15 sessions, Michael was attending weekly gay events, was less depressed, and was willing to put himself in anxiety-provoking situations to develop same-sex relationships.

The second case was Anne, a lesbian woman who was fearful of "coming out." Anne had negative judgments about lesbians. Rogers had her write down her thoughts about what it meant for her to be a lesbian. Some of her descriptions included "I couldn't have children," "I would be alienated from my family," "I would be discriminated against," and ultimately, "I would be lonely for the rest of my life" (Safren & Rogers, 2001, p. 639). With the use of disputation of negative thoughts, cognitive restructuring, and having Anne attend places where she would meet other women who were also lesbians, she was finally able to disclose her sexual orientation to her mother, sister, and friends.

Religious Groups and REBT/CBT

Earlier in his professional career, Albert Ellis (1962, 1980) expressed a very skeptical view of organized religion. Later, however, he admitted that over the years his views had changed (Ellis, 2000b). His newer stance was that it was not the religion per se, but rather the kind of beliefs regarding the religion that mattered. Ellis recognized the research demonstrating that the personal image of a loving and caring God may be emotionally healthy. He even conceded that REBT is most remarkably compatible with religious groups, particularly "benevolent religious philosophies of self-control and change, unconditional self-acceptance, high frustration tolerance, unconditional acceptance of others, [and] the desire rather than the dire need for achievement . . ." (Ellis, 2000a, p. 31). He even went so far as to encourage using scriptures as a part of the dialectic within therapy.

Christianity. There are a number of tenets in REBT/CBT that are most compatible with Christian values, such as the belief that all persons are created equal and that sins may be forgiven (Ellis, 2000a; Johnson, Ridley, & Nielsen, 2000; Waller, Trepka, Collerton, & Hawkins, 2010). In their clinical experience, DiGuiseppe, Robin, and Dryden (1990) found that clients who were having issues related to religious conflicts often presented with irrational beliefs concerning (a) demandingness, (b) low frustration tolerance (LFT), and (c) rating human worth. These authors offered clinical REBT strategies to help in disputing these irrational beliefs.

Consider a religious woman, Mrs. B., who came into therapy because she is depressed that her daughter just had an abortion. She said to the counselor that her thoughts were "My daughter should not, must not, have had the abortion" (DiGuiseppe et al., 1990, p. 359). Without disputing the client's belief in the Bible, or the woman's moral beliefs, the authors suggested that, among other things, even in the story of Adam and Eve in the Book of Genesis, God did not negate free will. It is an irrational belief to *demand* that someone MUST or MUST NOT do something.

Since one of the main tenets of REBT is that of human worth, when considering Mrs. B's near-condemnation of her daughter, DiGuiseppe et al. (2009) disputed her berating in a number of ways. In the Christian tradition, sins are forgivable. The authors reminded Mrs. B. of her belief that God is the final judge at death. They humorously asked her, "Did God call you up on the phone and say, 'I'm busy today, would you mind condemning a few people and start with your daughter'—that's what you're doing— you are playing God" (p. 363).

When clients present with guilt over continuing to violate one of their religious principles or commandments, DiGuiseppe et al. (1990) cautioned against simply relieving the guilt by disputing the client's feelings of worthlessness without looking at the low frustration tolerance for changing her or his behavior. They presented a case of a man who was having an extramarital affair. While they were able to decrease the unhealthy disturbed guilt, they challenged his belief that society was unfair to demand monogamy. When asked why he didn't follow the moral code, he responded, "Because I think I can't stand not to gratify myself" (p. 366). It was the LFT that would need to be disputed.

Johnson et al. (2000) also recognized the potential of using REBT with religiously oriented clients. They proposed a three-dimensional model of *religiously sensitive* therapy. The first dimension incorporates the necessary prerequisites for a counselor to deal effectively with a religiously oriented client such as familiarity with different religious cultures and perspectives, the counselor's own religious attitudes and beliefs, and the cognitive ability to appreciate the complexity of religious issues. The second dimension addresses the specific rituals or religious practices that might be used in a respectful way, even suggesting that "being disturbed is not God's intent and they will most likely become better to serve God and do God's will when they are less upset" (Johnson et al., 2000, p. 18). The third dimension is the evaluation of the effectiveness of the interventions by assessing attainment of the desired goals such as client satisfaction and motivation for change.

Judaism. Just as many tenets of REBT/CBT are compatible with Christianity, Pies (2011) identified a number of connections between rabbinical Judaism and REBT/CBT. Pies drew on rabbinical masters and Talmudic teachings to demonstrate seven common themes.

1. As in REBT, the Torah demands self-examination.
2. Both teach that self-mastery is a goal to be strived for but will never be fully achieved and one's emotions depend on cognitions.
3. Both place an emphasis on overcoming negative behaviors more so than simply achieving insight about the behaviors. Simply put, actions speak louder than words.
4. Both promote the importance of self-sufficiency and acceptance of discomfort as part of life.
5. Both require that individuals develop a tolerance of the behaviors of themselves and others.
6. Both recognize that happiness and unhappiness are not caused by external factors and can be controlled internally.
7. Both deemphasize the need for immediate gratification over more long-term self-fulfillment.

In using REBT/CBT with Orthodox Jews, Paradis, Cukor, and Friedman (2006) highlighted important beliefs and values that are shared by many Orthodox Jews and will need to be factored into treatment. In general, Orthodox Jews consider their religious and civil obligations as equal. They often value their religious community more important than mainstream American society. Many groups do not accept marriage to anyone who is not Orthodox. Family is of utmost importance, and the primary role of a woman is one to her family. Children must respect their parents and elders and not criticize them.

Johnson (2013) provided a case study of a Jewish couple who were struggling with their 22-year-old son who had recently announced to his parents that he was in a gay relationship with another Jewish man. Using REBT therapy, the couple's religious beliefs were identified. While affirming the Jewish values and recognizing the couple's desire to be grandparents, disputation centered around the *demanding* that their son *must not* be gay and the *awfulizing* the fact that they might not be grandparents. After only eight sessions, the couple was able to have a healthy rational disappointment regarding their son's relationship but a real acceptance that he was a gift from God.

Paradis et al. (2006) also pointed out that there is often a stigma attached to mental illnesses and it may be harder for a counselor who is not from within the Orthodox community. Rabbinical consultation is encouraged, especially when dating, marital, and birth control issues are the focus of treatment. In vivo or shame-attacking exercises might be harder if clients live in a predominantly Orthodox community. Still, these authors suggested that there are advantages of using REBT/CBT with members of the Orthodox community since it is generally shorter in duration and focused on improving symptoms so that the client is better able to fulfill her or his obligations to the family and community.

Islam. Members of the Islamic religion are referred to as *Muslims* (Abudabbeh & Hayes, 2006). These authors explained that the Islamic religion is traced back to the Prophet Mohammed (570–632 CE), who wrote Islam's sacred scriptural text, the Qur'an, and encouraged persons from the Arabian Peninsula to *surrender* (*Islam* means *surrender*) to the will of Allah. Although there is skepticism regarding counselors' understanding and respect of Islamic values, certain tenets of Islam, such as logical reasoning and an emphasis on education and consultation, are compatible with the tenets of REBT/CBT (Weinrach et al., 2004). On the other hand, other notions, such as the emphasis placed in individualism and self-determination in REBT/CBT, may be in conflict with the values of Islam (Beshai, Clark, & Dobson, 2013). A devout Muslim will interpret the *shoulds* and *should nots* in the Qur'an as definitives from Allah, and the REBT/CBT counselor must avoid challenging these religious beliefs, such as the belief that homosexuality is wrong (Beshai et al., 2013). At the same time, a devout Muslim may take solace even in times of great tragedy that the events are the will of Allah. However, just as it is true in Christianity and Judaism, there is much diversity within the Muslim community (Beshai et al., 2013; Hodge & Nadir, 2008). Notwithstanding, the centrality of the family is a core value to Muslims (Abudabbeh & Hays, 2006). There are many stipulations in the Qur'an and Sharia law regarding marriage, sexual intercourse, and contraception, but celibacy and monasticism are not acceptable (Johnson, 2013). A Muslim man may marry a woman who is a non-Muslim provided she is either Jewish or Christian, but a woman may only marry a Muslim man (Abudabbeh & Hays, 2006; Johnson, 2013). Because REBT/CBT is adaptable for work with families, issues regarding marital difficulties, and sexuality, this approach may be considered an appropriate match for a Muslim family or couple (Abudabbeh & Hays, 2006).

Johnson (2013) presented a case of a Muslim couple, Abdullah and Khadijah, who came to therapy. Abdullah wanted Khadijah to stop working outside their home. He believed that this was a requirement of Islam. The counselor was an REBT practitioner who respected their religious concerns. He suggested that the couple consult with an Islamic scholar who subsequently informed them that it was not a violation of the law. While Abdullah was willing to accept this judgment, he was fearful that his friends in the mosque would reject him and think that he was a failure as a man. After disputing such irrational beliefs, Abdullah came to realize that even if his friends would reject him, Allah would not. He focused his thoughts on a *hadith*, or saying of Mohammed, that his perseverance in prayer, despite disapproval of others, would gain him favor in heaven.

Recommendations for Counselors

For Hays (1995, 2009), REBT/CBT is an excellent fit for working with culturally diverse populations. REBT/CBT places an emphasis on the uniqueness of each individual and helps empower the client to make changes. This in turn contributes to developing a respectful therapeutic relationship. REBT/CBT's emphasis on specific behaviors rather than unconscious processes lessens the possibility of misunderstanding the counselor. Likewise, the REBT/CBT counselor has the opportunity to collaborate with the client by assessing the client's perception of the progress being made throughout the course of therapy. While emphasizing the strengths of REBT/CBT, Hays (1995, 2009) recognized that there are some limitations as well. Because REBT/CBT was developed in a Western society, notions such as independence and assertiveness that are valued in this society are often held in similarly high esteem by other cultures. Likewise, a counselor may not always inquire about cultural differences that the client may have in her or his background and upbringing.

- You will need to be conscious of assessing the individual and family needs with an emphasis on culturally respectful behavior in an effort to build rapport. This respect may mean that you will need to consider using fewer questions and being comfortable with hesitancies and silences.
- You should inquire about specific supports and strengths that a person may take pride in that are culturally related. Are there religious or spiritual rituals? Are there special talents or skills that you have that are part of your cultural heritage?

In some instances, when a person may believe it too boastful to answer directly, consider asking what someone else says about them. Ask the client to make a list of these strengths.

- Even though the *elegant solution* in REBT/CBT is to uncover underlying cognitive beliefs, you should first assess if the person believes that his or her presenting problem is related to cultural or external factors as well.
- When the activating event has an environmentally based factor, focus on helping the person gain personal strength such as communication skills building. Ask about self-care activities that may be inexpensive and culturally relevant.
- Again, although the focus of REBT/CBT is on challenging thoughts, if a client reports an experience of discrimination or oppression, do not minimize this. It is important to validate the client before examining other possible alternatives.
- Be conscious of the cultural differences between you and your client. You will want to find ways to emphasize that collaboration is important even when you may be challenging his or her cognitions.
- It may take more time for the culturally different person to be ready for cognitive restructuring. In the beginning, ask about how helpful the person's thoughts or beliefs may be. For example, a Muslim who lives in Boston may be fearful of being profiled by police. Rather than beginning with "What would be the worst thing if this were true?" Consider questioning, "How helpful is it to believe that?" Perhaps in the beginning, it may help the client be more cautious about the restaurant she or he goes into. You will need to assess the level of trust your client has with you before you dispute her or his irrational beliefs
- Be aware of the core cultural beliefs that your client may have. In many instances it will be better not to challenge them. For instance, in many Asian cultures, there is a strong emphasis on family and community (Iwamasa et al., 2006). An individual may be struggling because she or he has an opportunity to take a promotion that would entail moving to another state, but his family insists that he live closer to home to help take care of his elderly father. It is important that you show the client that you respect this more collectivist value.
- Help the client recognize that the list of culturally related strengths that she or he developed can be useful in helping develop more healthy beliefs or cognitions. An example may be the devout Latina woman who spoke about *familismo*. You may speak to her about the implication that she is valued by others.
- Try to speak with your client about weekly homework assignments that are congruent with the client's culture. Consider a religious person who is struggling with depression and has learned how to do Rational Emotive Imagery. The client has agreed to practice this each day. You ask, "What is something that you really enjoy doing?" The client may respond, "Reading a devotional book." You then ask, "What is something that you really, really don't like doing?" The client may respond, "Weeding my garden." You direct the client: "You will practice your imagery *before* reading your devotional book. If you do not, you will weed your garden for at least an hour."

In conclusion, I encourage prospective REBT/CBT counselors to reflect on their own personal beliefs and, perhaps, even implicit biases if they wish to become culturally competent providers. I encourage readers to consider your ethical responsibility to be sensitive to and learn about the challenges of multicultural counseling in a male-dominated, white-privileged society.

Summary

- While racial progress has been made, white privilege continues to exist in the United States.
- A culturally skilled counselor becomes aware of one's biases, understands clients without negative judgments, and actively develops strategies and skills in working with culturally different clients.
- Useful tools for counselors include a multicultural framework that is RESPECTFUL and nine cultural influences that they should be ADDRESSING.
- Research evidence showing applications to Latinos and Asian Americans was presented; research evidence showing REBT/CBT applications for LGBTQ populations was also presented.
- Although Ellis originally expressed a very skeptical view of organized religion, his views changed, and he came to see many adaptive aspects of spirituality.
- REBT/CBT was shown to be highly compatible with major world religions such as Christianity, Judaism, and Islam.
- Specific suggestions were given about how a culturally competent, contemporary counselor, who is a proponent of REBT/CBT, could integrate multicultural adaptations into his or her practice.

5

A Case Illustration
Using REBT/CBT

In this chapter, I share with you how clinicians coming from the REBT/ CBT orientation are sensitive to the developmental level of their clients and respectful of the therapeutic relationship. I provide a clinical case in detail and also offer brief illustrations using REBT/CBT with children and adolescents as well as emphasizing importance of the therapeutic alliance in working with this population.

The Case of Jessie

I begin with the fictitious case example of Jessie Anne. Jessie Anne is a 14-year-old biracial adolescent who is in the eighth grade. Her mother is Caucasian, and her father is African-American. She has a twin sister and an older brother who is in college and not living at home. She lived with both parents and her twin sister in the suburbs of Philadelphia until last year when her mother was placed in a residential program for eating disorders for a period of 6 months. During that time, her father assumed responsibilities as the primary caregiver. Recently, however, 2 months after her mother's return from the treatment facility, Jessie's father was hospitalized for a seizure and remained in a coma for 3 days. After recovery from the coma he was diagnosed with a brain tumor. He remains in the hospital, and her mother has now taken a more active role as the caregiver.

This past month Jessie's grades have fallen. She was an A-B student but is now receiving Cs and Ds. There is no suspicion of a learning disability, but her math teacher asked the school counselor to meet with Jessie since she has been neglecting her homework and had an outburst in class. She also had a fight in the cafeteria and received a detention for throwing her lunch at another student. The school counselor met with Jessie and the counselor suggested that Jessie receive outside counseling. Jessie agreed with the suggestion.

Session One: Meeting Jessie

Jessie presents to the outside counselor as outgoing and friendly but readily admits being angry and frustrated. Since her mother returned home, meals have been a struggle. Jessie understands that healthy eating is important, but she insists that her mother "goes overboard" and junk food is a "no-no!" During this first session, a number of issues emerge. Jessie and her twin are not identical. Her sister is more petite, lighter skinned, and built like her mother. The night before her father had his seizure, Jessie and her sister had an argument about body images. Jessie also suggested that she felt guilty and wondered if the argument had anything to do with her father's illness.

For the sake of this case illustration, Jessie's counselor is a white female in her middle 30s. She is a member of the Association of Behavioral and Cognitive Therapies (ABCT), who appreciates the importance in practicing from a culturally sensitive perspective and agrees with Wright and Davis's (1994) assertion that the "therapeutic relationship is an essential, interactive component of cognitive-behavioral therapy" (p. 42). She will be aware of building that relationship by keeping in mind the suggestions that they provided.

- I will strive to provide a safe and professional setting for my meeting with Jessie.
- I will treat Jessie with respect as a person.
- I will take Jessie's concerns seriously.
- I will remember to have Jessie's best interests in mind.
- I want to let Jessie know that I am competent.
- I want to give Jessie practical information.
- I will allow Jessie to make her own choices while keeping my information and suggestions at hand.
- I will try to stay flexible in my thinking about Jessie.

The counselor knows that REBT/CBT sessions are active and engaging from the very beginning. As Garfield (1989, 1995) noted, setting mutual goals builds the therapeutic relationship. Jessie sets up her goals. She admits that she wants to learn to control her anger. She also discusses the fact that she has some guilt about the fight with her sister the night before her father was taken to the hospital. Finally, she mentions that she does not think she is as attractive as her sister.

The counselor then proceeds to give a brief demonstration using a bottle of water and a bottle of soda. She shakes them both vigorously then asks Jessie which she would prefer to take. Jessie admitted that she liked soda but didn't want the one presented to her because "it might explode." The counselor proceeded to tell Jessie that anger unchecked could be like that bottle of soda. However, she assured Jessie that through her counseling sessions, she would help Jessie learn ways to recognize triggers that spark anger and develop.

The counselor continues by explaining the ABCs of REBT. She points out to Jessie that it is not so much the activating event (A) that causes Jessie's anger (C) but what she tells herself about the situation (B). She explores the cafeteria fight that began when another student told Jessie that it was her own fault that she failed the math test because she was lazy and had not handed in her assignments. Jessie was angry because the other student knew her mother was in the hospital and *should have* been more sensitive to that.

Rather than immediately disputing Jessie's *should have*, the counselor decided to explore a few *brain retrains* that Jessie could do to *Stop and Think* when she experiences the beginning of anger. Jessie comes up with suggestions that she writes on an index card:

- Count backwards from 10
- Walk away
- Breathe deeply and tell myself that this won't kill me
- Talk with a friend
- Write my feelings down
- Know that violence will only make things worse

Jessie agrees that between this session and the next she will write down any situation that made her angry.

Session Two: Jessie and Her Twin Sister

This counseling session begins with the counselor asking Jessie about situations that evoked anger since their last meeting. Jessie reports that she did write things down but the one situation that was most disturbing was between her and her sister. Her sister told Jessie that she was starting to gain weight and her clothes were getting too tight. Jessie did walk away and write in her journal, but on a scale of 1 to 10 she was still REALLY angry with her sister. She wanted to know what she could do.

The counselor is aware that she must be RESPECTFUL (see D'Andrea & Daniels, 2001) of the biracial issues for Jessie and believes that before delving into Jessie's negative and/or irrational beliefs, it would be important to teach Jessie how to use "I" statements. In *Ellisonian* language, this might be considered an *inelegant solution* but one that might help Jessie. In session, Jessie practiced saying, "When you say this **I feel angry because** you have more of Mom's features and don't seem to appreciate Dad's. I wish that you would be more sensitive to the fact that I do have more of his features."

Still, being RESPECTFUL does not deter the counselor from beginning to encourage Jessie from examining her cognitive distortions and/or irrational beliefs. Together they begin to explore some possibilities. Jessie agrees that sometimes she engages in what might be described as *mind reading* when she makes the conclusion that others are thinking negative thoughts about her. From this she tends to engage in *fortune telling* by predicting that things will always be the worse. She is not attractive and will never find a suitable boyfriend. This is *catastrophizing*.

The counselor recognizes this as an opportunity to point out Jessie's tendency to *musterbate* and *awfulize*. She encourages Jessie to dispute her irrational belief that others MUST think positively about her.

At the conclusion of this session the counselor invites Jessie to do a *shame attack*. Jessie says that she will try.

Session Three: Jessie and Dad

This session begins with Jessie reporting about her shame attack. She intentionally wore a pair of "outdated" gym shoes (otherwise known as *bobos*). The counselor asked Jessie what she said to herself to make this situation bearable. Jessie reported that she made it into kind of a game. She said to herself she was trying to reintroduce styles that might eventually make lots of money. Regardless, Jessie admitted that she recognized that what she told herself about a situation could affect her feelings about the situation. The counselor then moves to encourage Jessie to explore her guilt about her dad's condition.

The counselor believes that Jessie's willingness to follow through with this assignment suggests that the therapeutic relationship is developing and decides to challenge Jessie even further. She begins to talk with Jessie about her feelings of guilt. Did the fight that Jessie had with her sister cause her father's seizure? Worst case scenario, what if it did?

They put it in ABC terms:

A. I have a fight with my sister and my dad has a seizure (I did something wrong).
B. I MUST not do wrong things. Since I did, I am a bad daughter and sister.
C. I feel VERY guilty (on a scale of 1 to 10, Jessie reports an 11).

The counselor talks to Jessie more about *disputation*. (Jessie seems to be caught in an *All or Nothing* thinking pattern.) Were there times when you were a good daughter? Good sister? The counselor encourages Jessie to give actual examples. Jessie talks about how she likes to surprise her mom and dad on their anniversary. Last year she bought them tickets to a Phillies game. She does her chores around the house. She helps her sister with her homework.

This leads the counselor to talk about the difference between irrational guilt and a more rational sense of regret. What can Jessie say to herself to lessen her irrational guilt and turn it into more rational regret? Jessie comes up with this statement: "I am sorry I had the fight but I am still a good person. I am more than my actions."

The counselor gives Jessie a Thought Record such as Table 5.1 to keep for during the next week. Jessie agrees to this, and the counselor compliments Jessie on her willingness to continue working with her and congratulates her for the times she was a good daughter and sister.

Table 5.1   Example of a Thought Record

What happened?	My emotion or feeling	My negative thought	Evidence supporting the thought	Evidence contrary to the thought	Alternative thought	Different emotion

Sessions Four Through Seven: Jessie and Mom

Jessie appears more frustrated when she arrives for this session. When the counselor asks Jessie about it, she said that she had successfully completed one example on her Thought Record, but last night she and her mom had an argument. Like with her sister, the situation had to do with Jessie's weight. Jessie blurts out, "I can't stand it. She was anorexic and had to be hospitalized. We got along fine without her. All I want to do is eat what I want without having her nag me. I will never be as thin as she is. I hardly look like her. I think she must hate me!"

The counselor recognizes that there are a number of issues at play. They will not all be tackled in one session. The counselor recognizes that trying to have Jessie's best interest in mind and wanting her to be part of the decision-making process will strengthen the therapeutic relationship. The counselor then asks Jessie to prioritize her concerns. Over the next three sessions, they decide to deal with (a) body image, (b) racial differences, and (c) mom's approval.

Body Image. Although Jessie has more of her father's features, she is ambivalent about what the "ideal body" is that she wants. In session, the counselor has Jessie look through various magazines and comment on the models that she sees. Jessie notes that most are thin Caucasian women. She acknowledges that she doesn't identify with these pictures. The counselor then tells Jessie that she will bring in a copy of *Ebony Magazine* for the next session. They will look for differences.

The counselor turns to a related question. She asks Jessie, "Are you only your body?" The counselor wants Jessie to focus on some of her positive personal qualities. She asks Jessie to list what good qualities she has now and has shown in the past. She asks how her friends might describe her in a positive way. For her homework assignment she asks Jessie to complete self-affirmation index cards. On the first (I AM) card, she is to list statements about who she is. On the second (I CAN) card, she is to make statements about her potential. On the third (I WILL) card, she is to make statements about what she will do this week to make herself happy. She suggests that Jessie read them aloud in front of a mirror. She then challenges Jessie to sing them to a tune of one of her favorite songs. Jessie laughs at this. The counselor remarks that counseling can be fun.

Racial Differences.   Jessie reports that she couldn't think of how to put her self-affirmation statements to a song but she remembered hearing the lyrics to the song, "You Are So Beautiful to Me" in a school play. She Googled it and listened to Joe Cocker singing it. She imagined someone singing it to her. On her self-affirmation cards she wrote:

- I am a twin sister
- I am a student
- I am a daughter
- I can get good grades when I try
- I can play softball
- I can swim really well
- I will try to be less angry
- I will try to be nicer to my sister

Jessie and her counselor then began to look through copies of *Ebony Magazine.* Jessie immediately comments that the models are not as thin as the ones from the other magazines. The counselor replies that she has done some reading about cultural differences. She told Jessie that she found research indicating that African-American women repeatedly stated that a higher body weight was more acceptable and this did not impact their positive body image (Sanderson, Lupinski, & Moch, 2013). In other words, African-American women tend to be more comfortable with a higher body weight than women from other races/ethnicities. The counselor then directed Jessie to find pictures in the magazine that she thought were attractive. Jessie then made a collage from pictures and words that showed things she liked doing. She pasted them around her name, Jessie Anne, and gave the collage the title "I am black and beautiful." She remembered hearing this in the church she attends.

The counselor then leads Jessie through a Guided Image Imagery and Mindfulness Exercise on Body Image. (A copy of this is included on the website for this book.) She asks Jessie to practice this exercise each day.

Before ending this session, the counselor asks Jessie about her earlier statement about her mom hating her. Jessie admits that she really doesn't have any proof, so not much disputation is needed. Still, the counselor is aware that in the future Jessie might be willing to examine the more elegant solution that won't *demand* that her mom loves her but rather *prefers* so. The counselor is trying to be sensitive to Jessie's needs.

Session Eight: Will Dad Die?

The prognosis for Jessie's dad is not good. Jessie is tearful when she comes in for her session. She reports being angry and afraid. She doesn't know what she will be like if her dad dies. She realizes now that her argument with her sister did not cause the brain tumor. The tumor did not suddenly appear. The doctors said it had been growing for at least a year.

The counselor realizes that the future is uncertain. She begins to process Jessie's father's illness with her. Can she change her dad's prognosis? The counselor encourages Jessie to think about other things in her life that she could not change. Jessie mentions her family members and their move from Philadelphia to the suburbs. It is important to recognize that some things in life cannot be changed. But how we deal with them can. What are things that Jessie can do? Together they compile a list of options. The counselor is mindful that even if there were something that Jessie could do to change the situation, and she didn't do it, Jessie would need to develop unconditional self-acceptance.

While the ultimate reality of dad's possible death (Activating Event) is not going to change, the focus may need to shift to daily coping in the meantime. Disputing irrational beliefs might not be appropriate at this time. Grief is not solved in a session. It will be a longer process. Realizing this, the counselor speaks to Jessie about some short-term goals. She wants to help Jessie identify some positive coping strategies. She has Jessie talk about some of the good strategies she is using and some not-so-good strategies. She encourages Jessie to continue keeping her thought records.

Regarding her fears, the counselor asks Jessie what her greatest fear seems to be. Jessie's response is somewhat ambiguous, although she mentions that she can't imagine living without her dad. The counselor then inquires about spiritual, religious, or cultural supports she may have. Jessie reports that her family has other biracial friends and she attends a very diverse and liberal nondenominational church. The counselor suggests that these may be culturally related strengths that could be of benefit.

While this may not be the final session with Jessie, the counselor believes that from a common factors perspective, the therapeutic relationship is strong. She reminds Jessie that there will be ups and downs with her dad's illness. She also suggests that perhaps her mom and sister may want to do a session together with Jessie.

Rational Emotive Education and REBT/CBT Techniques for Children

At the Annual Conference of the Australian Psychological Society, which paid tribute to Albert Ellis, Bernard (2008), a colleague of Ellis, addressed the topic of why Ellis believed that REBT could easily be adapted for children. Ellis believed that children are born with the innate capacity to think irrationally. This irrationality is moderated when reasoning ability begins to emerge at Piaget's concrete operational stage around the age of 6. This logical reasoning develops more fully around age 12 with the emergence of the formal operational stage. This is important because when children or adults become extremely upset, their thinking is more reflective of Piaget's preconventional stage of thinking. When working with children, Bernard called for counselors to be guided by the stage a child may be in when doing disputations. In Jessie's case, she may revert to preconventional thinking when she is upset, and the counselor should be mindful of this fact.

Bernard (2004) suggested that when children are facing adversely emotional situations, they tend to revert to a preoperational stage of cognitive thinking. Characteristics of this stage include making conclusions that evidence may contradict, focusing on a detail that is taken out of context, and overgeneralization. In Jessie's case, she was magically thinking that her argument could have precipitated her father's illness. In the forward of Bernard's (2004) book, Ellis suggested that working with adolescents, children, and their parents can be difficult, but it is a task that a trained REBT counselor is prepared to undertake.

In teaching children to dispute irrational beliefs, different approaches have been suggested (Bernard, 2004; Bernard, Ellis, & Terjesen, 2006). The *didactic* style can be helpful in directly explaining the differences between irrational beliefs and rational beliefs. Consider this example from Jessie's case:

> So you tell me that you can't stand it when your mom goes on a rampage about eating healthy. Here it is today and you have survived this slight. I think that you are able to see that there really is no evidence to support your idea.

Another method of disputing irrational beliefs with children is the *Socratic* method. This style uses a series of questions. Here are examples of such questions:

> In examining your 14 years of life, can you find any evidence that you can't stand it when your sister starts to get on you about gaining weight? If there really isn't any evidence, what can you conclude?

Empirical disputation looks at the actual evidence to see if the child's inferences are based in reality. It is useful for children in the concrete stage of thinking (DiGiuseppe & Bernard, 2006). It can take the form of a simple experiment. For example, if Jessie reverts back to a concrete stage of thinking when she is upset, she may say that she never gets good grades. Her counselor may ask her to put a check mark next to subjects that she might get good grades in. Even if there are just a few check marks, the counselor could help her realize that even though she may be struggling with her grades at the moment, she still is able to get good grades.

In assessing the degree of emotional *upsetment* with children and adolescents, using an emotional thermometer is useful. For example, consider the thermometer in Table 5.2 in helping Jessie understand and describe how things might look differently if she could lessen her degree of anger such as in the fight she had with her sister.

Table 5.2   Degrees of Anger

	What happened first?	How might you feel?	What might you do?	What might happen?
	My sister told me I looked like I needed to lose weight.	Rage, fury	Swear, throw a book at her, and yell back.	My mother yelled and I would be punished.
		Medium anger	I say I am angry at things but don't swear or throw the book.	My sister doesn't listen, and I am upset, but I won't get punished.
		Annoyed	I say, "When you said that, I got angry. I wish you wouldn't tell me to lose weight."	My sister might even apologize.

©istockphoto/alxpin

Evidenced-Based Practice

In 2005, the American Psychological Association (APA) issued a policy statement recommending that clinicians utilize evidence-based interventions. Such *evidence-based practice* (EBP) was defined as "the integration of the best research evidence with clinical expertise" (American Psychological Association, 2005, p. 1). This generally implies that the treatment has been tested using randomized clinical trials (RTC) and relies on the use of treatment manuals (Beidas, Benjamin, Puleo, Edmunds, & Kendall, 2010). However, others (Duncan & Miller, 2006; Lambert, 1998) have pointed out that reliance on manualized treatments can tend to stifle creativity. The challenge for counselors is to find a balance between the two. I suggest one particular program that has been successful in working with children while balancing creativity with EBP is the Coping Cat Program (Kendall, Gosch, Furr, & Sood, 2008). Throughout the counselor's manual there are *flex* activities that allow the counselor flexibility and creativity while maintaining fidelity in presenting the material.

Coping Cat Program

The Coping Cat is an empirically supported manual-based CBT program for treatment of anxiety disorders in children ages 7 to 13 (Beidas et al., 2010; Kendall et al., 2008). This program consists of 16 sessions using the counselor manual (Kendall & Hedtke, 2006a) and a student workbook (Kendall & Hedtke, 2006b). The first eight sessions are psychoeducational when the children and adolescents learn to identify their thoughts, feelings, and bodily cues associated with those feelings. During these sessions, the counselor helps the child develop a *FEAR* plan (Feeling frightened? Expecting bad things? Actions and Attitudes that can help? Results and Rewards). Here I apply this to Jessie's fear that her dad might die.

> *Feeling frightened?* "Yes, I get a queasy stomach when I think about my dad's brain tumor."
>
> *Expecting bad things?* "Yes, I can't think straight in school, and I think I may fail this year in school and my family will think I am a big mess up."
>
> *Actions and Attitudes that can help?* "I can talk with my mother and sister as well as my school counselor. I could remember the good times we had together. I could also think about times when I used to get better marks. I could make sure I do my homework every night."
>
> *Results and Reward:* "I did do better on my math test and my teacher said that I would not fail this year. My mom was very proud, and she took my sister and me out to lunch at our favorite pizza place. I am still nervous about the summer, but I am keeping a journal and can bring it to you when I see you again."

There have been a number of randomized clinical trials demonstrating the efficacy of the Coping Cat program (Albano & Kendall, 2002; Schneider et al., 2013). In addition, Creed and Kendall (2005) examined the counselor alliance-building behaviors using the 16-week manualized CBT treatment. These authors found that collaboration and more informality were positively correlated to the clients' ratings of the alliance. Substance Abuse and Mental Health Services Administration (SAMHSA) recognized the Coping Cat treatment program as worthwhile and evidence based.

CBT/REBT Exercises With Children and Adolescents

I end with two brief exercises that I have adapted for use with children and adolescents.

Progressive Muscle Relaxation

Progressive muscle relaxation is an exercise that helps you relax both your mind and your body (Dolbier & Rush, 2012). It is a two-step process. The first step involves tensing various groups of muscles for about 5 seconds. This is followed by relaxing those muscles and contrasting the different sensations. While there are many scripts available for children, one that I have adapted is from Natal (http://www.natal.org.il/english/? CategoryID=274), Israel's Trauma Center for Victims of Terror and War.

By making this a game for children, it may distract them from worrying and help them feel more calm. (*Tensing muscles is in italics*, relaxing them is not.)

Legs: *Pretend that you are on the beach and walking barefoot on the sand. Try digging down as deep as you can but only with your toes. (Tense tense tense for 5 seconds)*

Next, lift your feet out of the sand. They feel so nice and comfortable.

Stomach: *Now pretend that a baby elephant is getting close to you and you think it is going to step on your belly. You tighten up your stomach muscles just in case it does. Make those muscles as tight as you can. (Tense tense tense for 5 seconds)*

Phew, the elephant is gone, so you can relax your stomach muscles again.

Arms and Shoulders: *Now pretend you're a lazy kitten slowly stretching itself. Stretch your arms high up above your head; lift your shoulders, move your arms out to your sides. (Tense tense tense for 5 seconds)*

Now relax your shoulders.

Neck: *Next, pretend that you're a turtle. Suddenly you see something scary and you disappear into your shell. Pull your shoulders up to your ears and push your head down in between your shoulders. (Tense tense tense for 5 seconds)*

The danger has passed. You can come out of your shell and enjoy the sunshine again.

Face: *Stretch your face into the widest smile you can—from ear to ear! Lift up your eyebrows . . . as high as you can. A fly is crawling on your nose and it tickles. Try to make it go away just by moving the muscles around your nose and your face. (Tense tense tense for 5 seconds).*

The fly has flown away, and your face can relax.

Being Mindful of the Present

I believe that helping anxious children focus on the present moment can be done without formal scripts. This can be done even with their pet dog (or cat) who doesn't mind being petted. Ask the child to pet her dog gently. Then have her do it closing her eyes. Ask the child to think about what the fur feels like.

You can ask an older child to look around the room and tell you three things she sees. Next have her close her eyes and tell you three things she hears. Then ask her to tell you three things that she is feeling right now.

Summary

- The educational tenets of REBT/CBT were introduced with a real focus on building the relationship following the model proposed by Wright and Davis (1994).
- Disputation and challenging of negative thoughts was done in a way that focused on Jessie's strengths.
- Completed homework assignments suggested that there was trust in the relationship.
- Complimenting Jessie helped build the relationship.
- Humor helped build the relationship.
- Examples using REBT/CBT techniques with children were provided.
- Two brief exercises were provided.

6

Conclusion

Throughout these chapters I have tried to show that REBT/CBT counselors have in fact, despite criticism to the contrary, always valued the client relationship. But it is a common factor that unfortunately has often been overlooked.

Yes, it is true that Carl Rogers surely emphasized unconditional positive regard. This is at the heart of person-centered approaches. Rogers (1957/2007) hypothesized that change will not occur outside of the relationship between the counselor and the client. In addition, unconditional positive regard is a necessary condition on the part of the counselor. He explained this as involving "as much as acceptance of ways in which he is inconsistent as of ways in which he is consistent" (Rogers, 1957/2007, p. 243).

But do not think for a minute that Albert Ellis and Aaron Beck weren't focused on their patients. They did care about them and took their concerns to heart. From early on in his career, Ellis paid attention to his clients. In actuality, it was precisely because he was paying such close attention to his clients that he was willing to abandon his psychoanalytic approach. He discovered that he was often wrong especially when it came to interpreting his patients' dreams. Ellis thought that many of his patients often resisted the psychoanalytic method, particularly free association. And Ellis (2010) believed that the process of psychoanalysis took too long. Still, Ellis would argue that helping a client develop unconditional self-acceptance is more critical than providing unconditional positive regard. By doing this, the counselor is actually emphasizing and enhancing the relationship without overreliance on the counselor.

In the same vein, Aaron Beck questioned some of the basic tenets of psychoanalysis and set out to examine them empirically. The prevailing notion in psychoanalysis at that time was that persons who were depressed were experiencing unconscious anger or rage toward a loved one. However, this hostility is not acceptable to the patient so it is repressed and blocked by a defense mechanism that redirects the hostility inward. In other words, this intrapsychic need to suffer or *retroflected hostility* was inevitable (see Beck, 2006, 2008; Smith, 2009). Beck believed that by doing dream analyses of patients who were depressed, he would uncover the hostility and empirically validate this notion.

However, he found contradictory evidence and reported that "these anomalies led me to a critical evaluation of the psychoanalytic theory of depression and ultimately of the entire structure of psychoanalysis" (Beck, Rush, Shaw, & Emery, 1979, p. ii). Rather, Beck began to realize that his depressed patients often had global negative distortions of their experiences. This led to the development of what is known today as CBT.

In the more recent "third wave" developments of CBT, practitioners of DBT and ACT purposely moved the therapeutic alliance front and center. Dimeff and Linehan (2001) explained that the early attempts to apply standard CBT to chronically suicidal patients with borderline personality disorder met with many difficulties. The major modification that was made was to add "radical acceptance and validation of clients' capabilities and behavioral functioning" (Dimeff & Linehan, 2001, p. 10) as central to DBT.

Similarly, in ACT, the counselor focuses on the therapeutic alliance. The client is not to be viewed as being flawed or damaged but as able to live a meaningful life despite unwanted experiences. Recall the mountain metaphor. The counselor has a unique view of the client's mountain even while climbing her or his own. The therapeutic alliance is collaborative rather than hierarchical (Lejuez, Hopko, Levine, Gholkar, & Collins, 2006).

You need not take on Ellis's or Beck's persona if you choose to practice REBT/CBT. I only encourage you to recognize that you may have many unique individuals cross your path during your practice as a counselor. Remember, you, too, are a unique individual with your own gifts and talents. Use these to help those persons who may have been damaged in other relationships. It isn't an irrational belief that the counseling relationship truly matters!

References

Abudabbeh, N., & Hays, P. A. (2006). Cognitive-behavioral therapy with people of Arab heritage. In P. A. Hays & G. Y. Iwamasa (Eds.), *Culturally responsive cognitive-behavioral therapy: Assessment, practice, and supervision* (pp. 141–160). Washington, DC: American Psychological Association.

Addis, M. E., Wade, W. A., & Hatgis, C. (1999). Barriers to dissemination of evidence-based practices: Addressing practitioners' concerns about manual-based psychotherapies. *Clinical Psychology: Science and Practice*, 6(4), 430–441.

Ahn, H., & Wampold, B. E. (2001). Where oh where are the specific ingredients? A meta-analysis of component studies in counseling and psychotherapy. *Journal of Counseling Psychology*, 48, 251–257. doi: 10.1037//O022-OI67.48.3.251

Albano, A. M., & Kendall, P. C. (2002). Cognitive behavioural therapy for children and adolescents with anxiety disorders: Clinical research advances. *International Review of Psychiatry*, 13, 129–134. doi: 10.1080/09540260220132644

Alford, B. A., & Beck, A. T. (1997). *The integrative power of cognitive therapy*. New York, NY: Guilford Press.

American Counseling Association. (2005). *ACA Code of Ethics*. Alexandria, VA: Author.

American Psychological Association. (2005, August). *Policy statement on evidence-based practice psychology*. Washington, DC: American Psychological Association.

American Psychological Association Task Force on Appropriate Therapeutic Responses to Sexual Orientation. (2009). *Report of the task force on appropriate therapeutic responses to sexual orientation*. Washington, DC: American Psychological Association. Retrieved from http://www.apa.org/pi/lgbt/resources/therapeutic-response.pdf

Arch, J. J., Ayers, C. R., Bakers, A., Almklov, E., Dean, D. J., & Craske, M. G. (2013). Randomized clinical trial of adapted mindfulness-based stress reduction versus group cognitive therapy for heterogeneous anxiety disorders. *Behavior Research and Therapy*, 51, 185–196.

Arredondo, P., Toporek, R., Brown, S. O., Jones, J., Locke, D. C., Sanchez, J., & Stadler, H. (1996). Operationalization of the multicultural counseling competencies. *Journal of Multicultural Counseling & Development*, 24(1), 42–78.

Arredondo, P., Tovar-Blank, Z. G., & Parham, T. A. (2008). Challenges and promises of becoming a culturally competent counselor in a social era of change and empowerment. *Journal of Counseling and Development, 86*(3), 261–268.

Axelrod, S. R., Perepletchikova, F., Holtzman, K., & Sinha, R. (2011). Emotion regulation and substance use frequency in women with substance dependence and borderline personality disorder receiving dialectical behavior therapy. *American Journal of Drug and Alcohol Abuse, 37,* 37–42. doi: 10.3109/00952990.2010.535582

Baer, R. A. (2003). Mindfulness training as a clinical intervention: A conceptual and empirical review. *Clinical Psychology: Science and Practice, 10,* 125–143. doi: 10.10093/clipsy/bpg015

Baer, R. A., Carmody, J., & Hunsinger, M. (2012). Weekly change mindfulness and perceived stress in a mindfulness-based stress reduction. *Journal of Clinical Psychology, 68,* 755–765. doi: 10.1002/jclp.21865

Baker, R. R., & Pickren, W. E. (2007). *Psychology and the Department of Veterans Affairs: A historical analysis of training, research, and advocacy.* Washington, DC: American Psychological Association.

Balsam, K. F., Martell, C. R., & Safren, S. S. (2006). Affirmative cognitive-behavioral therapy. In P. A. Hays & G. Y. Iwamasa (Eds.), *Culturally responsive cognitive-behavioral therapy: Assessment, practice, and supervision* (pp. 223–244). Washington, DC: American Psychological Association.

Bandura, A. (1974). Behavior therapy and the models of man. *American Psychologist, 29,* 859–869.

Bar, M. (2009). A cognitive neuroscience hypothesis of mood and depression. *Trends in Cognitive Science, 13,* 456–463. doi: 10. 1016/j.tics.2009.08.009

Barrett-Lennard, G. T. (1962). Dimensions of therapist response as casual factors in therapeutic change. *Psychological Monographs: General and Applied, 76,* 1–36.

Beauregard, M. (2009). Effect of mind on brain activity: Evidence from neuroimaging studies of psychotherapy and placebo effect. *Nordic Journal of Psychiatry, 63,* 5–16. doi: 10.1080/08039480802421182

Beck, A, T., Freeman, A., & Davis, D. D. (Eds.). (2004). *Cognitive therapy of personality disorders* (2nd ed.). New York, NY: Guilford Press.

Beck, A. T. (1963). Thinking and depression I: Idiosyncratic content and cognitive distortions. *Archives of General Psychiatry, 9,* 324–333.

Beck, A. T. (1964). Thinking and depression II: Theory and therapy. *Archives of General Psychiatry, 10,* 561–571. doi: 10.1176/appi.ajp.2008.08050721

Beck, A. T. (1976). *Cognitive therapy and the emotional disorders.* New York, NY: International Universities Press.

Beck, A. T. (2006). How an anomalous finding led to a new system of psychotherapy. *Nature Medicine, 12,* xiii–xv.

Beck, A. T. (2008). The evolution of the cognitive model of depression and its neurobiological correlates. *American Journal of Psychiatry, 165,* 969–977.

Beck, A. T., & Alford, B. A. (2009). *Depression: Causes and treatment* (2nd ed.). Philadelphia: University of Pennsylvania Press.

Beck, A., Rush, A. J., Shaw, B. F., & Emery, G. (1979). *Cognitive therapy of depression.* New York, NY: Guilford Press.

Becker, J. M., & Rosenfeld, J. G. (1976). Rational-emotive therapy—A study of initial therapy sessions of Albert Ellis. *Journal of Clinical Psychology, 32*, 872–876.

Beckham, E. (1989). Improvement after evaluation in psychotherapy of depression: Evidence of a placebo effect? *Journal of Clinical Psychology, 45*, 945–950.

Bedics, J. D., Atkins, D. C., Comtois, K. A., & Linehan, M. M. (2012). Treatment differences in the therapeutic relationship and introject during a 2-year randomized controlled trial of dialectical behavior therapy versus nonbehavioral psychotherapy experts for borderline personality disorder. *Journal of Consulting and Clinical Psychology, 80*(1), 66–77. doi: 10.1037/a0026113

Beidas, R. S., Benjamin, C. L., Puleo, C. M., Edmunds, J. M., & Kendall, P. C. (2010). Flexible applications of the coping cat program for anxious youth. *Cognitive and Behavioral Practice, 17*(2), 142–153.

Bernard, M. E. (2004). *The REBT therapist's pocket companion for working with children and adolescents.* New York, NY: Albert Ellis Institute.

Bernard, M. E. (2008, September). *Albert Ellis and the world of children.* Paper presented at the 43rd Annual Conference of the Australian Psychological Society, Tasmania.

Bernard, M. E., Ellis, A., & Terjesen, M. (2006). Rational-emotive behavioral approaches to childhood disorders: History, theory, practice, and research. In A. Ellis & M. E. Bernard (Eds.), *Rational emotive behavioral approaches to childhood disorders: Theory, practice and research* (pp. 3–84). New York, NY: Springer Science + Business Media.

Beshai, S., Clark, C. M., & Dobson, K. S. (2013). Conceptual and pragmatic considerations in the use of cognitive-behavioral therapy with Muslim clients. *Cognitive Therapy and Research, 37*, 197–206. doi: 10.1007/s10608-012-9450-y

Bhanji, A. (2011). Is it time we turn towards "third wave" therapies to treat depression in primary care? A review of the therapy and evidence with implications for counseling psychologists. *Counseling Psychology Review, 26*(2), 57–79.

Birnie, K., Speca, M., & Carlson, L. E. (2010). Exploring self-compassion and empathy in the context of mindfulness-based stress reduction (MBSR). *Stress and Health, 26*, 359–371. doi: 10.1002/smi.1305

Bodhi, B. (1998). *Toward a threshold of understanding.* Retrieved from http://www.accesstoinsight.org/lib/authors/bodhi/bps-essay_30.html

Bodhi, B. (2011a). *The noble eightfold path: The way to end of suffering.* Retrieved from http://www.accesstoinsight.org/lib/authors/bodhi/waytoend.htm

Bodhi, B. (2011b). What does mindfulness really mean? A canonical perspective. *Contemporary Buddhism, 12*, 19–39. doi: 10.1080/14639947.2011.564813

Bolton, J. B., McPoyle-Callahan, J. E., & Christner, R. W. (2012). Autism: School-based cognitive-behavioral interventions. In R. Mennuti, R. Christner, & A. Freeman (Eds.), *Cognitive-behavioral interventions in educational settings: A handbook for practice* (2nd ed., pp. 2469–2501). New York, NY: Taylor & Francis.

Bondolfi, G., Jermann, F., Van der Linden, M., Ger-Fabry, M., Bizzini, L., Rouget, B. W., . . . Bertschy, G. (2010). Depression relapse prophylaxis with mindfulness-based cognitive therapy: Replication and extension in the Swiss health care system. *Journal of Affective Disorders, 122*, 224–231. doi: 10.1016/j.jad.2009.07.007

Bordin, E. S. (1979). The generalizability of the psychoanalytic concept of the working alliance. *Psychotherapy: Theory, Research, and Practice, 16*, 252–260. doi: 10.1037/h0085885

Campbell, T. S., Labelle, L. E., Bacon, S. L., Faris, P., & Carlson, L. E. (2012). Impact of mindfulness-based stress reduction (MSBR) on attention, rumination, and resting blood pressure in women with cancer: A waitlist-controlled study. *Journal of Behavioral Medicine, 35*, 262–271. doi: 10.1007/s10865-011-9357-1

Castonguay, L. G., Golfried, M. R., Wiser, S., Raue, P. J., & Hayes, A. M. (1996). Predicting the effect of cognitive therapy for depression: A study of unique and common factors. *Journal of Consulting and Clinical Psychology, 64*, 497–504. doi: 10.1037/0022-006X.64.3.497

Chao, R. C. (2013). Race/ethnicity and multicultural competence among school counselors: Multicultural training, racial/ethnic identity, and color-blind racial attitudes. *Journal of Counseling & Development, 91*, 140–151. doi: 10.1002/j.1556-6676.2013.00082.x

Chen, C. P. (1995). Counseling applications of RET in a Chinese cultural context. *Journal of Rational-Emotive & Cognitive-Behavior Therapy, 13*(2), 117–129.

Chen, S. W.-H., & Davenport, D. S. (2005). Cognitive-behavioral therapy with Chinese American clients: Caution and modifications. *Psychotherapy: Theory, Research, Practice, and Training, 42*, 101–110.

Christodoulides, T., Dudley, R., Brown, S., Turkington, D., & Beck, A. T. (2008). Cognitive behaviour therapy in patients with schizophrenia who are not prescribed antipsychotic medication: A case series. *Psychology and Psychotherapy: Theory Research and Practice, 81*, 199–207. doi: 10.1348/147608x278295

Christopher, M. S. (2003). Albert Ellis and the Buddha: Rational soul mates? A comparison of rational emotive behavior therapy (REBT) and Zen Buddhism. *Mental Health, Religion, & Culture, 6*, 283–293. doi: 10.1080.1367467031000100975

Ciarrochi, J., & Bailey, A. (2008). *A CBT practitioner's guide to ACT: How to bridge the gap between cognitive behavioral therapy and acceptance and commitment therapy.* Oakland, CA: New Harbinger.

Claessens, M. (2010). Mindfulness based–third wave CBT therapies and existential-phenomenology: Friends or foes? *Existential Analysis: Journal of the Society for Existential Analysis, 21*(2), 295–304.

Clark, D. A., & Beck, A. T. (2010). *Cognitive therapy of anxiety disorders: Science and practice.* New York, NY: Guilford Press.

Conyers, L. M. (2002). Disability: An emerging topic in multicultural counseling. In J. Trusty, E. J. Looby, & D. S. Sandhu (Eds.), *Multicultural counseling: Context, theory and practice, and competence* (pp. 173–202). Huntington, NY: Nova Science.

Creed, T. A., & Kendall, P. C. (2005). Therapist alliance-building behavior within a cognitive-behavioral treatment for anxiety in youth. *Journal of Consulting and Clinical Psychology, 73*(3), 498–505. doi:10.1037/0022-006X.73.3.498

Cullen, C. (2008). Acceptance and commitment therapy (ACT): A third wave behavior therapy. *Behavioural and Cognitive Therapy, 36*, 667–673. doi: 10.1017/S1352465808004797

Dahl, J., Wilson, K. G., & Nilsson, A. (2004). Acceptance and commitment therapy and the treatment of persons at risk for long-term disability resulting from stress and pain symptoms: A preliminary randomized trial. *Behavior Therapy, 35*, 785–801.

D'Andrea, M., & Daniels, J. (2001). RESPECTFUL counseling: An integrative multidimensional model for counselors. In D. B. Pope-Davis & H. L. K. Coleman (Eds.), *The intersection of race, class, and gender in multicultural counseling* (pp. 417–466). Thousand Oaks, CA: Sage.

Dattilio, F. M. (2002). Homework assignments in couple and family therapy. *Psychotherapy in Practice, 58*, 535–547.

DiGiuseppe, R. (1991). A rational-emotive model of assessment. In M. Bernard (Ed.), *Using rational-emotive therapy effectively: A practitioner's guide* (pp. 151–172). New York, NY: Plenum Press.

DiGiuseppe, R., & Bernard, M. E. (2006). REBT assessment and treatment with children. In A. Ellis & M. E. Bernard (Eds.), *Rational emotive behavioral approaches to childhood disorders: Theory, practice and research* (pp. 85–114). New York, NY: Springer Science + Business Media.

DiGiuseppe, R., Leaf, R., & Linscott, J. (1993). The therapeutic relationship in rational-emotive therapy: Some preliminary data. *Journal of Rational-Emotive & Cognitive Behavior Therapy, 11*(4), 223–233.

DiGiuseppe, R., Robin, M. W., & Dryden, W. (1990). On the compatibility of rational-emotive therapy and Judeo-Christian philosophy: A focus on clinical strategies. *Journal of Cognitive Psychotherapy: An International Quarterly, 4*(4), 355–368.

Dimeff, L., & Linehan, M. M. (2001). Dialectical behavior therapy in a nutshell. *California Psychologist, 34*, 10–13.

Dobson, K. S. (1989). A meta-analysis of the efficacy of cognitive therapy for depression. *Journal of Consulting and Clinical Psychology, 57*, 414–419.

Dolbier, C. L. D., & Rush, T. E. (2012). Efficacy of abbreviated progressive muscle relaxation in a high-stress college sample. *International Journal of Stress Management, 19*, 48–68. doi: 10.1037/a0027326

Doll, B., Swearer, S. M., Collins, A. M., Chadwell, M. R., Dooley, K., & Chapla, B. A. (2012). Bullying and coercion: School-based cognitive-behavioral interventions. In R. Mennuti, R. Christner, & A. Freeman (Eds.), *Cognitive-behavioral interventions in educational settings: A handbook for practice* (2nd ed., pp. 339–375). New York, NY: Taylor & Francis.

Dreyfus, G. (2011). Is mindfulness present-centered and non-judgmental? A discussion of the cognitive dimensions of mindfulness. *Contemporary Buddhism, 12*(1), 41–54.

Dryden, W. (1991). Flexibility in RET: Forming alliances and making compromises. In M. Bernard (Ed.), *Using rational-emotive therapy effectively: A practitioner's guide* (pp. 133–149). New York, NY: Plenum Press.

Dryden, W., & Ellis, A. (2001). *Rational emotive behavior therapy: A handbook of cognitive-behavioral therapies* (2nd ed.). New York, NY: Guilford Press.

Duncan, B. L. (2002a). The founder of common factors: A conversation with Saul Rosenzweig. *Journal of Psychotherapy Integration, 12*, 13–31. doi: 10.1037//1053-0479.12.1.10

Duncan, B. L. (2002b). The legacy of Saul Rosenzweig: The profundity of the Dodo bird. *Journal of Psychotherapy Integration, 12*, 32–57. doi: 10.1037//1053-0479.12.1.32

Duncan, B. L., & Miller, S. (2000). *The heroic client.* San Francisco, CA: Jossey-Bass.

Duncan, B. L., & Miller, S. C. (2006). Treatment manuals do not improve outcomes. In J. C. Norcross, L. E. Beutler, & R. F. Levant (Eds.), *Evidence-based practices in mental health: Debate and dialogue on the fundamental questions* (pp. 140–148). Washington, DC: American Psychological Association.

Elkins, D. (2009). The medical model in psychotherapy: Its limitations and failures. *Journal of Humanistic Psychology, 49,* 66–84.

Elligan, D. (1997). Culturally sensitive integration of supportive and cognitive behavioral therapy in the treatment of a bicultural dysthymic patient. *Cultural Diversity and Ethnic Minority Psychology, 3,* 207–213.

Ellis, A. (1962). *Reason and emotion in psychotherapy: A new and comprehensive method of treating human disturbances.* Secaucus, NJ: Citadel Press.

Ellis, A. (1971a). *Growth through reason: Verbatim cases in rational emotive therapy.* Palo Alto, CA: Science and Behavior Books.

Ellis, A. (1971b). Emotional disturbance and its treatment in a nutshell. *Canadian Counselor, 5,* 168–171.

Ellis, A. (1973). *Humanistic psychotherapy: The rational approach.* New York, NY: McGraw-Hill.

Ellis, A. (1976). *The case against religion: A psychotherapist's view.* Cranford, NJ: American Atheist Press.

Ellis, A. (1977a). Fun as psychotherapy. In A. Ellis & Grieger, R. (Eds.), *Handbook of rational emotive therapy* (pp. 262–270). New York, NY: Springer.

Ellis, A. (1977b). Intimacy in psychotherapy. *Rational Living, 12,* 13–19.

Ellis, A. (1980). Psychotherapy and atheistic values: A response to A. E. Bergin's "Psychotherapy and Religious Values." *Journal of Counseling and Clinical Psychology, 48*(5), 635–639.

Ellis, A. (1989a). Comments on my critics. In M. E. Bernard & R. DiGiuseppe (Eds.), *Inside rational-emotive therapy* (pp. 199–233). San Diego, CA: Academic Press.

Ellis, A. (1989b). Using rational-emotive therapy (RET) as a crisis intervention: A single session with a suicidal client. *Individual Psychology, 45,* 75–81.

Ellis, A. (1993). Reflections on rational-emotive therapy. *Journal of Consulting and Clinical Psychology, 6,* 199–20.

Ellis, A. (2000a). Can rational emotive behavior therapy (REBT) be effectively used with people who have devout beliefs in God and religion? *Professional Psychology: Research and Practice, 29,* 29–33. doi:10.1037//0735-7028.31.1.29

Ellis, A. (2000b). Spiritual goals and spirited values in psychotherapy. *Journal of Individual Psychology, 56*(3), 277–284.

Ellis, A. (2002). *Overcoming resistance: A rational emotive behavior therapy integrated approach.* New York, NY: Springer.

Ellis, A. (2004). *The road to tolerance: The philosophy of rational emotive behavior therapy.* Amherst, NY: Prometheus Books.

Ellis, A. (2005). Discussion of Christine A. Padesky and Aaron T. Beck, "Science and Philosophy: Comparison of Cognitive and Rational Emotive Behavior Therapy." *Journal of Cognitive Psychotherapy: An International Quarterly, 19*(2), 181–185.

Ellis, A. (2007). General semantics and rational-emotive therapy: 1991 Alfred Korzybski memorial lecture. *ETC: A Review of General Semantics, 64,* 301–319.

Ellis, A. (2010). *Albert Ellis: All out—an autobiography.* Amherst, NY: Prometheus Books.

Ellis, A., & Grieger, R. (1977). *Handbook of rational emotive therapy.* New York, NY: Springer.

Ellis, A., & Harper, R. A. (1975). *A new guide to rational living.* North Hollywood, CA: Wilshire Book Co.

Ellis, A., & Lange, A. (1994). *How to keep people from pushing your buttons.* New York, NY: Carol.

Evans, S., Ferrando, S., Carr, C., & Haglin, D. (2011). Mindfulness-based stress reduction. *Psychotherapy, 18,* 553–558. doi: 10.1002/cpp.727

Exum, H. A., & Lau, E. Y. (1988). Counseling style preference of Chinese college students. *Journal of Multicultural Counseling and Development, 16*(2), 84–92.

Felder, J. N., Dimidjian, S., & Segal, Z. (2012). Collaboration in mindfulness-based cognitive therapy. *Journal of Clinical Psychology, 68,* 179–186. doi: 10.1002/jclp.21832

Fischer, A. R., Jome, L. M., & Atkinson, D. R. (1998). Reconceptualizing multicultural counseling: Universal healing conditions in a culturally specific context. *Counseling Psychologist, 26*(4), 525–588.

Fjorback, L. O., Arendt, M., Ørnbøl, E., Fink, P., & Walach, H. (2011). Mindfulness-based stress reduction and mindfulness-based cognitive therapy—A systematic review of randomized controlled trials. *Acta Psychiatrica Scandinavica, 124*(2), 102–119. doi: 10.1111/j.1600-0447.2011.01704.x

Flückiger, C., Del Re, A., Wampold, B. E., Symonds, D., & Horvath, A. O. (2012). How central is the alliance in psychotherapy? A multilevel longitudinal meta-analysis. *Journal of Counseling Psychology, 59,* 10–17. doi: 10.1037/a0025749

Forman, E. M., Herbert, J. D., Moitra, E., Yeomans, P. D., & Geller, P. A. (2007). A randomized controlled effectiveness trial of acceptance and commitment therapy and cognitive therapy for anxiety and depression. *Behavior Modification, 21,* 772–799. doi: 10.1177/0145445507302202

Forman, S. G., & Sharp, L. (2012). Substance-abuse prevention: School-based cognitive-behavioral approaches. In R. Mennuti, R. Christner, & A. Freeman (Eds.), *Cognitive-behavioral interventions in educational settings: A handbook for practice* (2nd ed., pp. 557–581). New York, NY: Taylor & Francis.

Freud, S. (1909). Analysis of a phobia of a five-year-old boy. In *The Pelican Freud Library (1977), Vol. 8, Case Histories 1,* 169–306.

Fuchs, T. (2004). Neurobiology and psychotherapy: An emerging dialogue. *Current Opinion in Psychiatry, 17,* 479–485.

Garfield, S. L. (1973). Basic ingredients or common factors in psychotherapy? *Journal of Consulting and Clinical Psychology, 41,* 9–12.

Garfield, S. L. (1989). The client-therapist relationship in rational-emotive therapy. In M. E. Bernard & R. DiGiuseppe (Eds.), *Inside rational-emotive therapy* (pp. 113–134). San Diego, CA: Academic Press.

Garfield, S. L. (1995). The client-therapist relationship in rational-emotive therapy. *Journal of Rational-Emotive & Cognitive-Behavior Therapy, 13,* 101–116.

Garfield, S. L., & Bergin, A. E. (1971). Therapeutic conditions and outcome. *Journal of Abnormal Psychology, 2,* 108–114.

Garland, S. N., Tamagawa, R., Todd, S. C., Speca, M., Carlson, L. E. (2013). Increased mindfulness is related to improved stress and mood following participation in a mindfulness-based stress reduction program in individuals with cancers. *Integrative Cancer Therapies, 12,* 31–40. doi: 10.1177/1534735412442370

Gay, P. (2006). *Freud: A life for our time.* New York, NY: Norton.

Gifford, E. V., Kohlenberg, B. S., Hayes, S. C., Antonuccio, D. O., Piasecki, M. M., Rasmussen-Hall, M. L., & Palm, K. M. (2004). Acceptance-based treatment for smoking cessation. *Behavior Therapy, 35*(4), 689–705.

Gilbert, P., & Leahey, R. L. (2007). Introduction and overview: Basic issues in the therapeutic relationship. In P. Gilbert & R. Leary (Eds.), *The therapeutic relationship in cognitive behavioral psychotherapies* (pp. 3–23). New York, NY: Routledge.

Godfrin, K. A., & van Heeringen, C. (2010). The effects of mindfulness-based cognitive therapy on recurrence of depressive episodes, mental health and quality of life: A randomized controlled study. *Behaviour Research and Therapy, 48,* 738–746. doi: 10.1016/j.brat.2010.04.006

Goldapple, K., Segal, Z., Garson, C., Lau, M., Bieling, P., Kennedy, S., & Mayberg, H. (2004). Modulation of cortical-limbic pathways in major depression: Treatment-specific effects of cognitive behavior therapy. *Archives of General Psychiatry, 61,* 34–41.

Goldin, E., & Bordan, T. (1999). The use of humor in counseling: The laughing cure. *Journal of Counseling Development, 77*(4), 405–410.

Gonzáles-Prendes, A. A., Hindo, C., & Pardo, Y. (2011). Cultural values integration in cognitive-behavioral therapy for a Latino with depression. *Clinical Case Studies, 10,* 376–394. doi: 10.1177/1534650111427075

Gosh, E. A., Flannery-Schroeder, E., & Brecher, R. J. (2012). Anxiety disorders: School-based cognitive-behavioral interventions. In R. Mennuti, R. Christner, & A. Freeman (Eds.), *Cognitive-behavioral interventions in educational settings: A handbook for practice* (2nd ed., pp. 2117–2160). New York, NY: Taylor & Francis.

Greenberg, G. (1997). Right answers, wrong reasons: Revisiting the deletion of homosexuality from the DSM. *Review of General Psychology, 1*(3), 256–270. doi: 10.1037/1089-2680.1.3.256

Greenson, R. R. (1965). The working alliance and the transference neurosis. *Psychoanalytic Quarterly, 34,* 155–179.

Greeson, J. M., Webber, D. M., Smoski, M. J., Brantley, J. G., Ekblad, M. J., Suarez, E. C., & Wolever, R. Q. (2011). Changes in spirituality partly explain health-related quality of life outcomes after mindfulness-based stress reduction. *Journal of Behavioral Medicine, 34,* 508–518. doi: 10.1007/s10865-011-9332-x

Grencavage, L. M., & Norcross, J. C. (1990). Where are the commonalities among the therapeutic common factors? *Professional Psychology: Research and Practice, 21,* 372–378.

Grosse Holtforth, M., & Castonguay, L. G. (2005). Relationship and techniques in cognitive-behavioral therapy: A motivational approach. *Psychotherapy: Theory, Research, Practice, Training.* 42, 443–455. doi: 10.1037/0033-3204.42.4.443

Grossman, P., Niemann, L., Schmidt, S., & Walach, H. (2004). Mindfulness-based stress reduction and health benefits: A meta-analysis. *Journal of Psychosomatic Research,* 57, 35–43. doi: 10.1016/S0022-399(03)00573-7

Gutiérrez, O., Luciano, C., Rodríguez, M., & Fink, B. C. (2004). Comparison between an acceptance-based and a cognitive-control-based protocol for coping with pain. *Behavior Therapy,* 35, 767–783.

Hanh, T. N. (1992). *Peace is every step: The path of mindfulness on everyday living.* New York, NY: Bantam Books.

Hardy, G., Cahill, J., & Barkham, M. (2007). Active ingredients of the therapeutic relationship that promote client change. In P. Gilbert & R. Leary (Eds.), *The therapeutic relationship in cognitive behavioral psychotherapies* (pp. 24–42). New York, NY: Routledge.

Hayes, S. C. (2004a). Acceptance and commitment therapy and the new behavior therapies: Mindfulness, acceptance, and relationship. In S. C. Hayes, V. Follette, & M. Linehan (Eds.), *Expanding the cognitive behavior tradition.* New York, NY: Guilford Press.

Hayes, S. C. (2004b). Acceptance and commitment therapy: Relational frame theory, and the third wave of behavioral and cognitive therapies. *Behavior Therapy,* 35, 639–665.

Hayes, S. C. (2010). *The ACT Model & Approach* [DVD]. Eau Claire, WI: CMI/Premier Education Solutions.

Hayes, S. C., Masuda, A., Bissett, R., Luoma, J., & Guerrero, L. F. (2004). DBT, FAP, and ACT: How empirically oriented are the new behavior therapy technologies? *Behavior Therapy,* 35, 35–54.

Hayes, S. C., Strosahl, K. D., & Wilson, H. G. (2012). *Acceptance & commitment therapy: The process and practice of mindful change* (2nd ed.). New York, NY: Guilford Press.

Hays, P. (1995). Multicultural applications of cognitive-behavior therapy. *Professional Psychology: Research and Practice,* 26(3), 309–315.

Hays, P. (1996). Addressing the complexities of culture and gender in counseling. *Journal of Counseling and Development,* 74(4), 332–338.

Hays, P. (2009). Integrating evidence-based practice, cognitive-behavior therapy, and multicultural therapy: Ten steps for culturally competent practice. *Professional Psychology: Research and Practice,* 40, 354–360. doi: 10.1037/a0016250

Helms, J. E. (1994). How multiculturalism obscures racial factors in the therapy process: Comment on Ridley et al. (1994), Sodowsky et al. (1994), Ottavi et al. (1994), and Thompson et al. (1994). *Journal of Counseling Psychology,* 14(2), 162–165.

Helms, J. E., & Carter, R. T. (1997). How multiculturalism obscures races and culture as different aspects of counseling competency. In D. B. Pope-Davis & H. L. K. Coleman (Eds.), *Multicultural counseling competencies* (pp. 60–79). Thousand Oaks, CA: Sage.

Henderson, V. P., Clemow, L., Massion, A. O., Hurley, T. G., Druker, S., & Hébert, J. R. (2012). The effects of mindfulness-based stress reduction on psychosocial outcomes and quality of life in early-stage breast cancer patients: A randomized trial. *Breast Cancer Research and Treatment, 131*, 99–109. doi: 10.1007/s10549-011-1738-1

Hendricks, A., Cohen, J. A., Mannarino, A. P., & Debliner, E. (n.d.). *Your very own TF-CBT workbook.* Retrieved from http://ego.thechicagoschool.edu/s/843/images/editor_documents/childadolescent/TF-CBT%20workbook.pdf

Herbert, J. D., & Gaudiano, B. A. (2005). Moving from empirically supported treatment lists to practice guidelines in psychotherapy: The role of the placebo concept. *Journal of Clinical Psychology, 61*, 893–908. doi: 10.1002/jclp.20133

Herek, G. M., Gillis, J. R., & Cogan, J. C. (1999). Psychological sequelae of hate-crime victimization among lesbian, gay, and bisexual adults. *Journal of Consulting and Clinical Psychology, 67*(6), 945–951.

Hixson, L., Hepler, B. B., & Kim, M. O. (2011). The white population: 2010: 2010 Census Briefs. Washington, DC: United States Census Bureau. Retrieved from http://www.census.gov/prod/cen2010/briefs/c2010br-05.pdf

Hobbs, N. (1962). Sources of gain in psychotherapy. *American Psychologist, 17*, 741–747.

Hodge, D. R., & Nadir, A. (2008). Moving toward culturally competent practice with Muslims: Modifying cognitive therapy with Islamic tenets. *Social Work, 53*, 31–41.

Hollon, S. D., & Beck, A. T. (1994). Cognitive and cognitive-behavioral therapies. In A. E. Bergin & S. L. Garfield (Eds.), *Handbook of psychotherapy and behavior change* (pp. 428–466). New York, NY: Wiley.

Hollon, S. D., DeRubeis, R. J., Shelton, R. C., Amsterdam, J. D., Salomon, R. M., & O'Reardon, J. P. (2005). Prevention of relapse following cognitive therapy vs. medications in moderate to severe depression. *Archives of General Psychiatry, 2*, 417–422.

Horvath, A. O. (2005). The therapeutic relationship: Research and theory: An introduction to the special issue. *Psychotherapy Research, 15*, 3–7. doi: 10.1080/10503300512331339143

Horvath, A. O., Del Re, A. C., Flückiger, C., & Symonds, D. (2011). Alliance in psychotherapy. *Psychotherapy, 48*, 9–16. doi: 10.1037/a0022186

Horvath, A. O., & Greenberg, L. S. (1989). Development and validation of the Working Alliance Inventory. *Journal of Counseling Psychology, 36*, 223–233. doi: 10.1037/0022-0167.36.2.223

Horvath, A. O., & Symonds, B. D. (1991). Relation between working alliance and outcome in psychotherapy: A meta-analysis. *Journal of Counseling Psychology, 38*(2), 139–149. doi: 10.1037//0022-0167.38.2.139

Howells, K. (2010). The "third wave" of cognitive-behavioural therapy and forensic practice. *Criminal Behaviour and Mental Health, 20*, 251–300. doi: 10.1002/cbm

Hubble, M. A., Duncan, B. L., Miller, S. D., & Wampold, B. E. (2010). Introduction. In B. L. Duncan, S. D. Miller, B. E. Wampold, & M. A. Hubble (Eds.), *The heart and soul of change: Delivering what works in therapy* (pp. 23–46). Washington, DC: American Psychological Association.

Hyer, L., & Kramer, D. (2004). CBT with older patients: Alterations and the value of the therapeutic alliance. *Psychotherapy: Theory, Research, Practice, Training, 41,* 26–29. doi: 10.1037/0033-3204.41.3.276

Interian, A., & Díaz-Martínez, A. M. (2007). Consideration for culturally competent cognitive-behavioral therapy for depression with Hispanic patients. *Cognitive and Behavioral Practice, 14,* 84–97.

Iwamasa, G. Y., Hsia, C., & Hinton, D. (2006). Cognitive-behavioral therapy with Asian Americans. In P. A. Hays & G. Y. Iwamasa (Eds.), *Culturally responsive cognitive-behavioral therapy: Assessment, practice, and supervision* (pp. 117–140). Washington, DC: American Psychological Association.

Johnson, S. A. (2013). Using REBT in Jewish, Christian, and Muslim couples counseling in the United States. *Journal of Rational-Emotive & Cognitive Behavioral Therapy, 31,* 84–92. doi: 10.1007/s10942-013-0161-4

Johnson, W. B., Ridley, C. R., & Nielsen, S. L. (2000). Religiously sensitive rational behavior therapy: Elegant solutions and ethical risks. *Professional Psychology: Research and Practice, 31,* 14–20. doi: 10.103/0735-7028.31.1.14

Jokić-Begić, N. (2010). Cognitive-behavioral therapy and neuroscience: Towards closer integration. *Psychological Topics, 19,* 235–254.

Kabat-Zinn, J. (1982). An outpatient program in behavioral medicine for chronic pain patients based on the practice of mindfulness meditation: Theoretical considerations and preliminary results. *General Hospital Psychiatry, 4,* 33–47.

Kabat-Zinn, J. (2003). Mindfulness-based interventions on context: Past, present, and future. *Clinical Psychology: Science and Practice, 10,* 144–156. doi: 10.1093/clipsy/bpg016

Kabat-Zinn, J. (2005). *Coming to our senses: Healing ourselves and the world though mindfulness.* New York, NY: Hyperion.

Kabat-Zinn, J. (2009, March 26). Opening to our lives: Jon Kabat-Zinn's science of mindfulness with Krista Tippett (Radio interview). Retrieved from http://www .onbeing.org/program/opening-our-lives/138/extraaudio?embed=1

Kabat-Zinn, J. (2011). Some reflections on the origins of MBSR, skillful means, and the trouble with MAPS. *Contemporary Buddhism, 12,* 281–306. doi: 10.1080/14639947.2011.564844

Kabat-Zinn, J., Lipworth, L., & Burney, R. (1985). The clinical use of mindfulness meditation for the self-regulation of chronic pain. *Journal of Behavioral Medicine, 8,* 163–190.

Kabat-Zinn, J., Wheeler, E., Light, T., Skillings, A., Scharf, M. J., Cropley, T. G., . . . Bernhard, J. D. (1998). Influence of a mindfulness mediation-based stress reduction intervention on rates of skin clearing in patients with moderate to severe psoriasis undergoing phototherapy (UVB) and photochemotherapy (PUVA). *Psychosomatic Medicine, 60,* 625–632.

Kendall, P. C., Gosch, E., Furr, J. M., & Sood, E. (2008). Flexibility within fidelity. *Journal of American Academy of Child and Adolescent Psychiatry, 47,* 987–993. doi: 10.1097/CHI.0b013e31817eed2f

Kendall, P. C., & Hedtke, K. A. (2006a). *Cognitive-behavioral therapy for anxious children: Therapist manual* (3rd ed.). Ardmore, PA: Workbook.

Kendall, P. C., & Hedtke, K. A. (2006b). *The coping cat workbook* (2nd ed.). Ardmore, PA: Workbook.

Kirsch, I. (2005). Placebo psychotherapy: Synonym or oxymoron? *Journal of Clinical Psychology, 61*, 791–803. doi: 10.1002/jclp.20126

Kluckhohn, C., & Murrary, H. A. (Eds.). (1948). *Personality in nature, society, and culture.* New York, NY: Knopf.

Koons, C. R., Robins, C. J., Tweed, J. L., Lynch, T. R., Gonzalez, A. M., Morse, J. Q., . . . Bastian, L. A. (2001). Efficacy of dialectical behavior therapy in women veterans with borderline personality disorder. *Behavior Therapy, 32*, 371–390.

Kumari, V., Fannon, D., Peters, E., Ffytche, D. H., Sumich, A. L., Premkumar, P., . . . Kuipers, E. (2011). Neural changes following cognitive therapy for psychosis: A longitudinal study. *Brain, 134*, 2396–2407. doi: 10.1093/awr154

Kurtz, R. R., & Grummon, D. L. (1972). Different approaches to the measurement of therapist empathy and their relationship to therapy outcomes. *Journal of Consulting and Clinical Psychology, 39*, 106–115. doi: 10.1037/h0024480

Kuyken, W., Byford, S., Taylor, R. S., Watkins, E., Holden, E., White, K., . . . Teasdale, J. D. (2008). Mindfulness-based cognitive therapy to prevent relapse in recurrent depression. *Journal of Consulting and Clinical Psychology, 76*(6), 966–978. doi: 10.1037/a0013786

Lambert, M. J. (1992). Implications of outcome research for psychotherapy integration. In J. C. Norcross & M. R. Goldfried (Eds.), *Handbook of psychotherapy integration* (pp. 94–129). New York, NY: Basic Books.

Lambert, M. J. (1998). Manual-based treatment and clinical practice: Hangman of life or promising development? *Clinical Psychology: Science and Practice, 5*, 391–395.

Lambert, M. J. (2005). Early response in psychotherapy: Further evidence for the importance of common factors rather than "placebo effects." *Journal of Clinical Psychology, 61*, 855–869. doi: 10.1002/jclp.20130

Lambert, M. J., & Barley, D. E (2001). Research summary on the therapeutic relationship and psychotherapy outcome. *Psychotherapy, 38*, 357–361. doi: 10.1037/0033-3204.38.4.357

Lambert, M. J., & Ogles, B. M. (2004). The efficacy and effectiveness of psychotherapy. M. J. Lambert (Ed.), *Bergin and Garfield's handbook of psychotherapy and behavior change* (5th ed., pp. 139–193). New York, NY: Wiley.

Lazarus, A. A. (1989). The practice of rational-emotive therapy. In M. E. Bernard & R. DiGiuseppe (Eds.), *Inside rational-emotive therapy* (pp. 95–112). San Diego, CA: Academic Press.

Ledesma, D., & Kumano, H. (2009). Mindfulness-based stress reduction and cancer: A meta-analysis. *Psycho-Oncology, 18*(6), 571–579. doi: 10.1002/pon.1400

Lejuez, C. W., Hopko, D. R., Levine, S., Gholkar, R., & Collins, L. M. (2006). The therapeutic alliance in behavior therapy. *Psychotherapy: Theory, Research, Practice, Training, 42*, 456–468. doi: 10.1037/0033-3204.42.4.456

Lin, Y. (2001). The application of cognitive-behavioral therapy to counseling Chinese. *American Journal of Psychotherapy, 55*(4), 46–58.

Linehan, M. (1987). Dialectical behavioral therapy: A cognitive behavioral approach to parasuicide. *Journal of Personality Disorders, 4,* 328–333.

Linehan, M. (1993a). *Cognitive-behavioral treatment of borderline personality disorders.* New York, NY: Guilford Press.

Linehan, M. (1993b). *Skills training manual for treating borderline personality disorder.* New York, NY: Guilford Press.

Linehan, M. (2012). *Experts in search of a common ground.* National Harbor, MD: Association for Behavioral and Cognitive Therapies Convention.

Linehan, M., Armstrong, H. E., Suarez, A., Allmon, D., & Heard, H. L. (1991). Cognitive-behavioral treatment of chronically parasuicidal borderline patients. *Archives of General Psychiatry, 48,* 1060–1064.

Linehan, M., Comtois, K. A., Murray, A. M., Brown, M. Z., Gallop, R. J., Heard, L. L., . . . Lindenboim, N. (2006). Two-year randomized controlled trial and follow-up of dialectical behavior therapy vs therapy experts for suicidal behaviors and borderline personality disorder. *Archives of General Psychiatry, 63,* 757–766.

Linehan, M., Dimeff, L. A., Reynolds, S. K., Comtois, K. A., Welch, S., Heagerty, P., & Kivlanhan, D. R. (2002). Dialectical behavior therapy versus comprehensive validation therapy plus 12-step for the treatment of opioid dependent women meeting criteria for borderline personality disorder. *Drug and Alcohol Dependence, 67,* 13–26.

Linehan, M., Schmidt, H., Dimeff, L. A., Craft, J. C., Kanter, J., & Comtois, K. A. (1999). Dialectical behavior therapy for patients with borderline personality disorder and drug dependence. *American Journal on Addiction, 8,* 279–292.

Longmore, R. J., & Worrell, M. (2007). Do we need to challenge thoughts in cognitive behavior therapy? *Clinical Psychology Review, 27,* 173–187. doi: 10.1016/j.cpr.2006.08.001

Lowe, S. M., & Mascher, J. (2001). The role of sexual orientation in multicultural counseling: Integrating bodies of knowledge. In J. C. Ponteratto, J. M. Casas, L. A. Suzriki, C. M. Alexander (Eds.), *Handbook of multicultural counseling* (2nd ed., pp. 755–778). Thousand Oaks, CA: Sage.

Luborsky, L., Crits-Christoph, P., Alexander, L., Margolis, M., & Cohen, M. (1983). Two helping alliance methods for predicting outcomes of psychotherapy: A counting signs vs. global rating method. *Journal of Nervous and Mental Disease, 179,* 480–491.

Lynch, T. R., Chapman, A. L., Rosenthal, M. Z., Kuo, J. R., & Linehan, M. (2006). Mechanisms of change in dialectical behavioral therapy: Theoretical and empirical observations. *Journal of Clinical Psychology, 62,* 459–480.

Lynch, T. R., & Cuper, P. (2010). Dialectical behavior therapy. In N. Kazantzis, M. A. Reinike, & A. Freeman (Eds.), *Behavior theories in clinical practice* (pp. 218–243). New York, NY: Guilford Press.

Ma, A. H., & Teasdale, J. D. (2004). Mindfulness-based cognitive therapy for depression: Replication and exploration of differential relapse prevention effects. *Journal of Consulting and Clinical Psychology, 72,* 31–40. doi: 10.1037/0022-0022-006X.72.1.31

Mahoney, M. J., & Gabriel, T. J. (1987). Psychotherapy and the cognitive sciences: An evolving alliance. *Journal of Cognitive Therapy, 1,* 39–59.

Makedon, A. (1996). *What multiculturalism should not be*. Chicago, IL: Chicago State University. Retrieved from http://alexandermakedon.com/articles/multiculturalism.html

Marmar, C. R., Weiss, D. S., & Gaston, L. (1989). Toward validation of the California therapeutic alliance rating system. *Psychological Assessment, 1*, 46–52.

Martin, D. J., Garske, J. P., & Davis, M. K. (2000). Relation of the therapeutic alliance with outcome and other variables: A meta-analytic review. *Journal of Consulting and Clinical Psychology, 68*, 438–450. doi: 10.1037/0022-006X.68.3.438

Matchim, Y., Armer, J. M., & Stewart, B. R. (2011). Effects of mindfulness-based stress reduction (MBSR) on health among breast cancer survivors. *Western Journal of Nursing Research, 33*, 996–1016. doi: 10.1177/0193945910385363

McIntosh, P. (1995). White privilege: Unpacking the invisible knapsack. Retrieved from http://amptoons.com/blog/files/mcintosh.html

Mennuti, R. B., Bloomgarden, A., Mathison, J., & Gabriel, N. (2012). Adolescents with eating disorders: School-based cognitive-behavioral interventions. In R. Mennuti, R. Christner, & A. Freeman (Eds.), *Cognitive-behavioral interventions in educational settings: A handbook for practice* (2nd ed., pp. 275–303). New York, NY: Taylor & Francis.

Miller, G., Yang, J., & Chen, M. (1997). Counseling Taiwan Chinese in America: Training issues for counselors. *Counselor Education and Supervision, 37*(1), 22–34.

Mills, D. H., & Zytowski, D. G. (1967). Helping relationships: A structural analysis. *Journal of Counseling Psychology, 3*, 193–197.

Mishlove, J., & Ellis, A. (1995). Philosophy in psychotherapy with Albert Ellis, Ph.D. *Thinking allowed, conversations on the leading edge of knowledge and discovery*. Retrieved from http://www.intuition.org/txt/ellis.htm

Montes, S. (2013, November 25). The birth of the neuro-counselor? *Counseling Today*, 2–8.

Mulligan, C. A., & Christner, R. W. (2012). Selective mutism: Cognitive-behavioral interventions. In R. Mennuti, R. Christner, & A. Freeman (Eds.), *Cognitive-behavioral interventions in educational settings: A handbook for practice* (2nd ed., pp. 187–214). New York, NY: Taylor & Francis.

Muran, J. C., Gorman, B. S., Safran, J. D., Twining, L., Samstag, L. W., & Winston, A. (1995). Linking in-session change to overall outcome in short-term cognitive therapy. *Journal of Consulting and Clinical Psychology, 63*, 651–657. doi: 10.1037/0022-006X.63.4.651

Nelson, J. K. (2007). Laugh and the world laughs with you: An attachment perspective on the meaning of laughter in psychotherapy. *Clinical Social Work Journal, 36*, 41–49. doi: 10.1007/s10615-007-0133-1

Nielsen, S. L., Johnson, W. B., & Ellis, A. (2001). *Counseling and psychotherapy with religious persons: A rational emotive behavior therapy approach*. Mahwah, NJ: Lawrence Erlbaum.

Olendzki, A. (2011). The construction of mindfulness. *Contemporary Buddhism, 1*, 55–70. doi: 10.1080/14639947.2011.564817

Organista, K. (2006). Cognitive-behavioral therapy with Latinos and Latinas. In P. A. Hays & G. Y. Iwamasa (Eds.), *Culturally responsive cognitive-behavioral therapy: Assessment, practice, and supervision* (pp. 73–96). Washington, DC: American Psychological Association.

Organista, K. C., & Muñoz, R. F. (1996). Cognitive behavior therapy with Latinos. *Cognitive and Behavioral Practice, 3*, 255–270.

Öst, L. (2008). Efficacy of the third wave of behavioral therapies: A systematic review and meta-analysis. *Behaviour Research and Therapy, 46*(3), 296–321. doi: 10.1016.j.brat.2007.12.005

Pack-Brown, S. P., Thomas, T. L., & Seymour, J. M. (2008). Infusing professional ethics into counselor education programs: A multicultural/social justice perspective. *Journal of Counseling & Development, 86*(3), 296–302.

Padesky, C. A., & Beck, A. T. (2003). Science and philosophy: Comparison of cognitive therapy and rational emotive behavior therapy. *Journal of Cognitive Psychotherapy, 17*, 211–224.

Pantalone, D. W., Iwamasa, G. Y., & Martell, C. R. (2009). Cognitive-behavioral therapy with Asian Americans. In P. A. Hays & G. Y. Iwamasa (Eds.), *Culturally responsive cognitive-behavioral: Assessment, practice, and supervision* (pp. 117–140). Washington, DC: American Psychological Association.

Paquette, V., Lévesque, J., Mensour, B., Leroux, J.-M., Beaudoin, G., Bourgouin, P., Beauregard, M. (2003). "Change the mind and you can change the brain": Effects of cognitive-behavioral therapy on the neural correlates of spider phobia. *Neuroimage, 18*, 401–409. doi: 10.1016/S1053-8119(02)00030-7

Paradis, C. M., Cukor, D., & Friedman, S. (2006). Cognitive-behavioral therapy with Orthodox Jews. In P. A. Hays & G. Y. Iwamasa (Eds.), *Culturally responsive cognitive-behavioral therapy: Assessment, practice, and supervision* (pp. 161–176). Washington, DC: American Psychological Association.

Petersen, C. L., & Zettle, R. D. (2009). Treating inpatients with comorbid depression and alcohol use disorders: A comparison of acceptance and commitment therapy versus treatment as usual. *Psychological Record, 59*, 521–536.

Pies, R. (2011). The Judaic foundations of rational-emotive behavioral therapy. *Mental Health, Religion, & Culture, 14*(5), 459–472.

Plum, S., & Hebblewaite, P. (2013). The "third wave" of cognitive behavioral therapy (CBT)—Can it be integrated into a Christian context? Retrieved from http://www.mindandsoul.info/Articles/232757/Mind_and_Soul/Resources/Articles/Mindfulness/Mindfulness_and_CBT.aspx1

Pope, M. (2002). Counseling individuals from the lesbian and gay cultures. In J. Trusty, E. J. Looby, & D. S. Sandhu (Eds.), *Multicultural counseling: Context, theory and practice, and competence* (pp. 201–218). Huntington, NY: Nova Science.

Pope-Davis, D. B., & Coleman, H. L. K. (2007). *Multicultural counseling competencies: Assessment, education, training, & supervision.* Thousand Oaks, CA: Sage.

Raue, P. J., Goldfried, M. V., & Barkham, M. (1997). The therapeutic alliance in psychodynamic-interpersonal and cognitive-behavioral therapy. *Journal of Consulting and Clinical Psychology, 65*, 582–587. doi: 10.1037/0022-006X.65.4.582

Rector, N. A., Zuroff, D. C., & Segal, Z. V. (1999). Cognitive change and the therapeutic alliance: The role of technical and nontechnical factors in cognitive therapy. *Psychotherapy, 36*, 320–328. doi: 10.1037/h0087739

Richardson, T. Q., & Jacob, E. J. (2002). Contemporary issues in multicultural counseling. In J. Trusty, E. J. Looby, & D. S. Sandhu (Eds.), *Multicultural counseling: context, theory and practice, and competence* (pp. 31–45). Huntington, NY: Nova Science.

Richman, J. (1996). Points of correspondence between humor and psychotherapy. *Psychotherapy, 4*, 560–566.

Robbins, C. J., Keng, S., Ekblad, A. G., & Brantley, J. G. (2011). Effects of mindfulness-based stress reduction on emotional experience and expression: A randomized controlled trial. *Journal of Clinical Psychology, 68*, 117–131. doi: 10.1002/jclp.20857

Rogers, C. (1957/2007). The necessary and sufficient conditions of therapeutic personality change. *Psychotherapy, Theory, Research, Training, 44*, 240–248. doi 10.1037/0022-006X.60.6.827

Roll, S., Millen, L., & Martinez, R. (1980). Common errors in psychotherapy with Chicanos: Extrapolations from research and clinical experience. *Psychotherapy: Theory, Research, and Practice, 17*(2), 158–168.

Rosenzweig, S. (1936/2002). Some implicit common factors in diverse methods of psychotherapy. *Journal of Psychotherapy Integration, 12*, 412–415. doi: 10.1037//1053-0479.12.1.5

Rosselló, J., Bernal, G., & Rivera-Medina, C. (2008). Individual and group CBT and IPT for Puerto Rican adolescents with depressive symptoms. *Cultural Diversity and Ethnic Minority Psychology, 14*(3), 234–245. doi: 10.1037/1099-9809.14.3.234

Ruiz, F. J. (2012). Acceptance and commitment therapy versus traditional cognitive behavioral therapy: A systematic review and meta-analysis of current empirical evidence. *International Journal of Psychology & Psychological Therapy, 12*, 333–357.

Rush, A. J., & Beck, A. T. (1978). Cognitive therapy of depression and suicide. *American Journal of Psychotherapy, 32*(2), 201–219.

Safren, A., & Rogers, T. (2001). Cognitive-behavioral therapy with gay, lesbian, and bisexual clients. *Psychotherapy in Practice, 57*(5), 629–643.

Salvio, M., Beutler, L. E., Wood, J. M., & Engle, D. (1992). The strength of the therapeutic alliance in three treatments for depression. *Psychotherapy Research, 21*, 31–36.

Sanderson, S., Lupinski, K., & Moch, P. (2013). Is black really beautiful: Understanding body image perceptions of African American females. *Journal of Black Studies, 44*, 496–507. doi: 10.1177/0021934713497059

SB 1172. (April 9, 2012). *Sexual orientation change efforts.* California.

Schneider, S., Blatter-Meunier, J., Herren, C., In-Albon, T., Adornetto, C., Meyer, A., & Lavallee, K. L. (2013). The efficacy of a family-based cognitive behavioral treatment for separation anxiety disorder in children aged 8–13: A randomized comparison with a general anxiety program. *Journal of Consulting and Clinical Psychology, 81*(5), 932–940. doi: 10.1037/a0032678

Segal, Z. V., Bieling, P., Young, T., MacQueen, G., Cooke, R., Martin, L., . . . Levitan, R. (2010). Antidepressant monotherapy vs. sequential pharmacotherapy and mindfulness-based cognitive therapy, or placebo, for relapse prophylaxis in recurrent depression. *Archives of General Psychiatry, 67*, 1256–1264.

Segal, Z. V., Williams, J. M. G., & Teasdale, J. D. (2002). *Mindfulness-based cognitive therapy for depression: A new approach to preventing relapse.* New York, NY: Guilford Press.

Shallcross, L. (2012, September). Proof positive. *Counseling Today, 55*(3), 28–37.

Siddique, J., Chung, J. Y., Brown, C. H., & Miranda, J. (2012). Comparative effectiveness of medication in a randomized controlled trial of low-income young minority women with depression. *Journal of Consulting & Clinical Psychology, 80*, 995–1006. doi: 10.1037/a0030452

Siegle, G. J., Carter, C. S., & Thase, M. (2006). Use of fMRI to predict recovery from unipolar depression with cognitive behavior therapy. *American Journal of Psychiatry, 163*, 735–738.

Skinner, B. F. (1985). Cognitive science and behaviorism. *British Journal of Psychology, 76*, 291–301.

Smith, D. B. (2009). The doctor is in. *American Scholar*, pp. 1–10.

Smith, M. L., & Glass, G. V. (1977). Meta-analysis of psychotherapy outcome studies. *American Psychologist, 32*, 752–760.

Smith, T. B., & Richards, P. S. (2002). Multicultural counseling in spiritual and religious contexts. In J. Trusty, E. J. Looby, & D. S. Sandhu (Eds.), *Multicultural counseling: Context, theory and practice, and competence* (pp. 105–128). Huntington, NY: Nova Science.

Speight, S. L., Myers, L. J., Cox, C. I., & Highlen, R. S. (1991). A redefinition of multicultural counseling. *Journal of Counseling & Development, 70*, 29–36.

Sperry, R. W. (1993). The impact and promise of the cognitive revolution. *American Psychologist, 48*, 878–885. doi: 10.1037/003-066X.48.8.878

Springer, J. M. (2012). Acceptance and commitment therapy: Part of the "third wave" in the behavioral tradition. *Journal of Mental Health Counseling, 34*(3), 205–212.

Sterba, R. (1934). The fate of the ego in analytic therapy. *International Journal of Psychoanalysis, 15*, 117–126.

Stiles, W. B., Agnew-Davies, R., Hardy, G. E., Barkham, M., & Shapiro, D. A. (1998). Relations of the alliance with psychotherapy outcome: Findings in the Sheffield Psychotherapy project. *Journal of Consulting and Clinical Psychology, 66*, 791–802. doi: 10.1037/0022-006X.66.5.791

Stiles, W. B., Shapiro, D. A., & Elliott, R. (1986). Are all psychotherapies equivalent? *American Psychologist, 41*, 165–180. doi: 10.1037/0003-066X.41.2.165

Storaasli, R. D., Kraushaar, B., Wilson, K. G., & Emrick, C. (2007). Convention, tradition, and the new wave: Assessing clinician identity in behavior therapy. *Behavior Therapist, 30*(7), 149–155.

Strupp, H. H. (1973a). On the basic ingredients of psychotherapy. *Journal of Consulting and Clinical Psychology, 1*, 1–8.

Strupp, H. H. (1973b). The interpersonal relationship as a vehicle for therapeutic learning. *Journal of Consulting and Clinical Psychotherapy, 41*, 13–15.

Sue, S. (1977). Community mental health services to minority groups: Some optimism, some pessimism. *American Psychologist, 32*, 616–624.

Sue, S. (1983). Ethnic minority issues in psychology. *American Psychologist, 38*, 583–592.

Sue, D. W. (2001). Multidimensional facets of cultural competence. *Counseling Psychologist, 29*, 790–821. doi: 10.1177/0011000001296002

Sue, D. W., Arredondo, P., & McDavis, R. J. (1992). Multicultural counseling competencies and standards: A call to the profession. *Journal of Counseling & Development, 70*, 477–486.

Sue, D. W., Bernier, J. E., Durran, A., Feinberg, L., Pedersen, P., Smith, E. J., & Vasquez-Nuttall, E. (1982). Position paper: Cross-cultural counseling competencies. *Counseling Psychologist, 10*(2), 45–52.

Sultanoff, S. M. (1992, July/August). The impact of humor in the counseling relationship. *Laugh It Up, Publication of the American Association for Therapeutic Humor*, 1. Retrieved from http://www.humormatters.com/articles/therapy2.htm

Summers, R. F., & Barber, J. P. (2003). Therapeutic alliance as a measurable psychotherapy skill. *Academic Psychiatry, 27*(3), 160–165.

Szentagotai, A., David, D., Lupu, V., & Cosman, D. (2008). Rational emotive behavior therapy versus cognitive therapy versus pharmacotherapy in the treatment of major depressive disorder: Mechanisms of change analysis. *Psychotherapy Theory, Research, Practice, Training, 45*(4), 523–538. doi: 10.1037/a0014332

Teasdale, J. D., & Chaskalson, M. (2011a). How does mindfulness transform suffering? I: The nature and origins of dukkha. *Contemporary Buddhism, 12*, 89–102. doi: 10.1080/14639947.2011.564824

Teasdale, J. D., & Chaskalson, M. (2011b). How does mindfulness transform suffering? II: The nature and origins of dukkha. *Contemporary Buddhism, 12*, 103–124. doi: 10.1080/14639947.2011.564826

Teasdale, J. D., Segal, Z., V., Williams, J. M., Ridgeway, V. A., Soulsby, J. M., & Lau, M. A. (2000). Prevention of relapse/recurrence in major depression by mindfulness-based cognitive therapy. *Journal of Consulting and Clinical Psychology, 68*, 615–623. doi: 10.1037//0022-006X.68.4.615

Tee, J., & Kazantzis, N. (2011). Collaborative empiricism in cognitive therapy: A definition and theory for relationship construct. *Clinical Psychology: Science and Practice, 18*, 47–61.

Thompson, C. E., & Neville, H. A. (1999). Racism, mental health, and mental health practice. *Counseling Psychologist, 27*, 155–223. doi: 10.1177.00110000992772001

Twohig, M. P., Hayes, S. C., Plumb, J. C., Pruitt, L, D., Collins, A. B., & Hazlett-Stevens, H. (2010). A randomized clinical trial of acceptance and commitment therapy versus progressive relaxation training for obsessive-compulsive disorder. *Journal of Counseling and Clinical Psychology, 78*, 705–716.

Twohig, M. P., & Woods, D. W. (2004). A preliminary investigation of acceptance and commitment therapy and habit reversal as a treatment for trichotillomania. *Behavior Therapy, 35*, 803–820.

Vontress, C. E. (1971). Racial differences: Impediments to rapport. *Journal of Counseling Psychology, 18*(1), 7–13.

Waller, R., Trepka, C., Collerton, D., & Hawkins, J. (2010). Addressing spirituality in CBT. *Cognitive Behavior Therapist, 3*, 95–106. doi: 10.1017/S175440X10000073

Waltz, T. J., & Hayes, S. C. (2010). Acceptance and commitment. In N. Kazantzis, M. A. Reinecke, & A. Freeman (Eds.), *Cognitive and behavioral strategies in clinical practice* (pp. 148–192). New York, NY: Guilford Press.

Wampold, B. (2010). *The great psychotherapy debate: Models, methods, and finding*. Mahwah, NJ: Taylor & Francis.

Wampold, B. E., Mondin, G. W., Moody, M., Stich, F., Benson, K, & Ahn, H. (1997). A meta-analysis of outcome studies comparing bona fide psychotherapies: Empirically, "all must have prizes." *Psychological Bulletin, 122*, 203–215. Retrieved from https://umdrive.memphis.edu/mpmrtens/public/CPSY%20 8200/Wampold%20et%20al.,%201997.pdf

Watson, J. C., & Geller, S. M. (2005). The relation among the relationship conditions, working alliance, and outcome in both process-experiential and cognitive-behavioral psychotherapy. *Psychotherapy Research, 15*, 25–33, doi: 10.1080/10503300512331327010

Weiler-Timmins, E. M. (2012). Lesbian, gay, bisexual, transgendered and questioning (LGBTQ) youth: School climate, stressors, and interventions. In R. Mennuti, R. Christner, & A. Freeman (Eds.), *Cognitive-behavioral interventions in educational settings: A handbook for practice* (2nd ed., pp. 503–529). New York, NY: Taylor & Francis.

Weinrach, S. G., Dryden, W., DiMattia, D. J., Doyle, K. A., Maclaren, C., O'Kelly, M., & Malkinson, R. (2004). Post–September 11th perspectives on religion, spirituality, and philosophy in the personal and professional lives of selected REBT cognoscenti. *Journal of Counseling & Development, 82*, 426–438.

Weinrach, S. G., & Thomas, K. R. (2002). A critical analysis of the multicultural counseling competencies: Implications for the practice of mental health counseling. *Journal of Mental Health Counseling, 24*(1), 20–35.

Wessler, R. A., & Wessler, R. L. (1980). *The principles and practice of rational-emotive therapy*. San Francisco, CA: Jossey-Bass.

Williams, J. M. G., & Kabat-Zinn, J. (2011). Mindfulness: Diverse perspectives on its meaning, origins, and multiple applications at the intersection of science and dharma. *Contemporary Buddhism, 12*, 1–18. doi: 10.1080/14639947.2011.564811

Winter, D. A., & Watson, S. (1999). Personal construct psychotherapy and the cognitive therapies: Different in theory but can they be differentiated in practice? *Journal of Constructivist Psychology, 12*, 1–11. doi: 10.1080/107205399266190

Wolpe, J., & Rachman, S. (1960). Psychoanalytic "evidence": A critique based on Freud's case of little Hans. *Journal of Nervous and Mental Disease, 130*(8), 135–148.

Wright, J. H., & Davis, D. (1994). The therapeutic alliance in cognitive-behavioral therapy: Patient perceptions and therapist responses. *Cognitive and Behavioral Practice*, *1*, 25–45.

Zurowski, B., Kordon, A., Weber-Fahr, W., Voderholzer, U., Kuelz, A., Freyer, T., . . . Fritz, H. (2012). *Relevance of orbitofrontal neurochemistry for the outcome of cognitive-behavioral therapy in patients with obsessive-compulsive disorder.* doi: 10.1007/s00406-012-0304-0

Index

Figures and tables are indicated by f or t following the page number.

About the Author

Diane J. Shea, PhD, is an Associate Professor for the Graduate Program in Counseling Psychology at Holy Family University, Philadelphia, Pennsylvania. She is a Nationally Certified Psychologist, a PA Certified School Psychologist, and a Licensed Professional Counselor. In addition to her academic credentials, she is a broadly experienced human services provider. She was the founding director of Bethany House, a group home in New York for homeless teenage mothers and their babies. Her expertise also includes providing clinical services, managing clinical staff, and providing individual and family services for adolescents in the Juvenile Justice System.

⑤SAGE research**methods**

The essential online tool for researchers from the
world's leading methods publisher

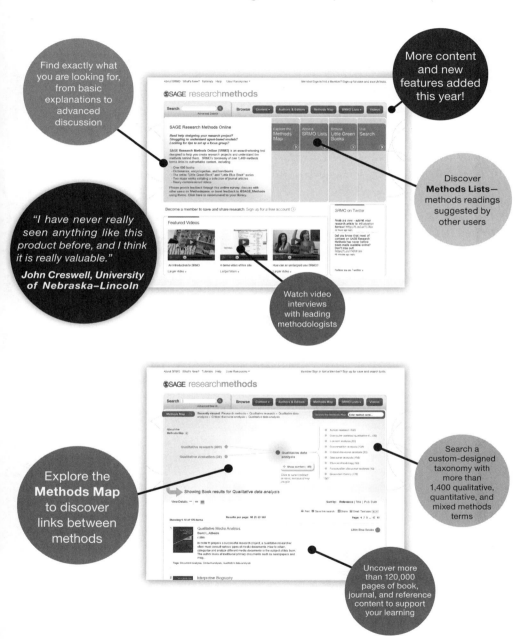

Find exactly what you are looking for, from basic explanations to advanced discussion

More content and new features added this year!

Discover **Methods Lists**— methods readings suggested by other users

"*I have never really seen anything like this product before, and I think it is really valuable.*"
John Creswell, University of Nebraska–Lincoln

Watch video interviews with leading methodologists

Explore the **Methods Map** to discover links between methods

Search a custom-designed taxonomy with more than 1,400 qualitative, quantitative, and mixed methods terms

Uncover more than 120,000 pages of book, journal, and reference content to support your learning

Find out more at
www.sageresearchmethods.com